jazz singer's HANDBOOK

michele weir

Jazz singing is one of the joys of my life.

Few other art forms invite the depth of personal expression and creativity inherent in jazz singing; it is a deeply rewarding music.

The goal of the *Jazz Singer's Handbook* is to inspire you to find your own unique voice as a vocal jazz artist, and to provide the necessary information to help you perform with confidence and integrity.

If you're a professional or aspiring professional jazz singer wanting to expand your creative palette and improve your skills in jazz singing, this book is for you. Or, if you are a classroom or private instructor looking for specific information and methods to guide your students in this idiom, read on!

Section I, "The Art of Jazz Singing" explores the creative and expressive possibilities in jazz singing. Section II, "The Mastery of Jazz Singing" provides information on the more technical aspects of being a jazz singer. Combined, the two sections will help you to become a complete vocal jazz musician, both artistically and professionally.

I wish you the best of luck with your jazz singing and hope that it will be as rewarding for you as it has been for me!

Alfred

CD Track Listing

1. Look for the Silver Lining (key of B♭)

2. Look for the Silver Lining (key of D♭)

3. Indian Summer (key of E♭)

4. Indian Summer (key of G)

5. The Love Nest (key of C)

6. The Love Nest (key of E♭)

7. After You've Gone (key of F)

8. After You've Gone (key of A♭)

9. My Honey's Lovin' Arms (key of E♭)

10. My Honey's Lovin' Arms (key of G)

11. Emotional Mood

12. Stylistic Tools

13. Melodic Variation

14. Phrasing; back/forward phrasing and phrasing over the bar line

15. Phrasing; space

16. Phrasing; rubato

17. Swing; laying back

18. Swing; rhythmic choices

19. Swing; preach singing

20. Swing; drums and voice counting beats of measure

21. Turnaround Intros (major keys)

22. Turnaround Intros (minor keys)

23. Vamp Intros (major keys)

24. Vamp Intros (minor keys)

25. Pedal Tone Intros (major keys)

26. Pedal Tone Intros (minor keys)

27. Miscellaneous Intros (major keys)

28. Miscellaneous Intros (minor keys)

29. Tag Endings; 2 and 3 time tags

30. Vamp Endings

31. Endings for Ballads

32. Chart 1: Route 66

33. Chart 2: Summertime

34. Chart 3: Fly Me to the Moon

35. Chart 4: God Bless the Child

36. Chart 5: One Note Samba

37. Arrangement 1: The Love Nest

38. Arrangement 2: The Love Nest

39. Count offs

Contents

About the Author

A faculty member at the University of California, Los Angeles (UCLA) since 1996, Michele Weir is a former member of the Grammy-nominated vocal group, "Phil Mattson and the PM Singers." Michele's vocal arrangements have been performed by groups including New York Voices, Beachfront Property, M-Pact, Chanticleer, and Voice Trek, and her orchestral arrangements have been performed by regional orchestras such as the Buffalo, Cincinnati and Pacific Symphonies. Michele has worked extensively as a pianist, including touring with singer Bobby Vinton.

Her compositions have been featured on the Shari Lewis TV show, "The Charlie Horse Music Pizza," and her educational vocal group arrangements are published with Hal Leonard, Heritage Jazz Press, Lindalamama, MichMusic, and U.N.C. Jazz Press among others.

An internationally respected jazz clinician, her recent presentations include the World Choral Symposium, the American Choral Directors Association and the International Association for Jazz Education conferences. Michele served as music supervisor for the foreign language versions of the Dreamworks film, "Prince of Egypt" in Mexico, Greece, Portugal, Denmark, Thailand and Japan. Her "Vocal Improvisation" educational book/CD is widely available and her CD release with guitarist, Bruce Forman is titled, "The Sound of Music."

www.micheleweir.com

Acknowledgments

Thank you very much to those who generously offered their thoughts and ideas as this book was being written: Kris Adams, Jennifer Barnes, Wendi Bourne, Mike Campbell, Jack Daro, Rosana Eckert, Jamie Findley, Bob Florence, Cathy Segal-Garcia, Matt Harris, Nina Harris, Christine Helferich, Tamir Hendelman, Diane Hubka, Clay Jenkins, Ellen Johnson, Kristin Korb, Rachel LeBon, Mirja Makela, Connaitre Miller, Tom Miller, Chris Neville, Kate Reid, Jamie Shew, John Stowell, Dave Stroud, Tom Warrington, Dick Weller, Judy Wexler, Sunny Wilkinson, Sharon Yazowski.

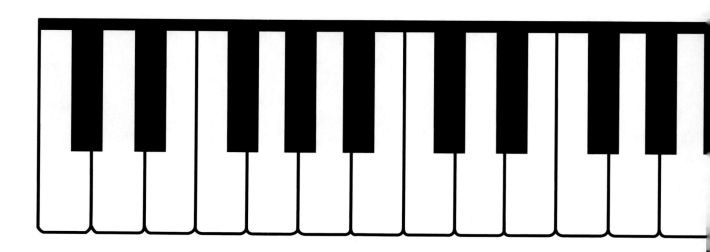

How to Use This Book

This book can be used by reading it cover to cover, or by skipping around to the chapters that are most pertinent for you at any given time. The CD is provided both to demonstrate various musical concepts and to allow you to practice singing specific exercises which are provided at the conclusion of most chapters. *Whether you do the suggested exercises or not depends on your experience level and personal preference.*

There are five songs in Chapter 1 which will be used throughout the book in conjunction with certain exercises: "Look for the Silver Lining," "Indian Summer," "The Love Nest," "After You've Gone," and "My Honey's Lovin' Arms." I recommend that you begin your use of this book by familiarizing yourself with these songs; the CD provides demonstration and accompaniment tracks for their practice.

It is assumed that you already have knowledge of note names, intervals, scales, triads and other basic musical information such as fermatas, ritards, and so on. Appendix I contains a summary of basic musical information for your reference as needed. Also, on the bottom of this page there is a representation of a piano keyboard. *You are encouraged to use this as a tool in the event you don't have access to a real piano.*

Having at least some knowledge of jazz chords and progressions is ideal, although it's not necessary. Appendix II contains a catalog of jazz chord types, for your reference. Appendix III is devoted to recommendations of specific publications which would be useful sources for reference or further study. And finally, if at any time you're in doubt about the meaning of a certain word or phrase, refer to the index to find its definition.

Do Yourself a Favor:

Learn Basic Jazz Piano!

Taking the time to learn to play a little bit of jazz piano is something you will never regret! The vast majority of professional jazz musicians have at least basic jazz piano skills. Knowing your way around the piano is truly an asset: it allows you to help yourself

learn tunes, transpose, check chord changes for accuracy, devise intros and endings, practice scat singing, and so on. Learning to play simple jazz chords with nice voicings is not difficult! Refer to Appendix III for suggested publications relating to jazz piano.

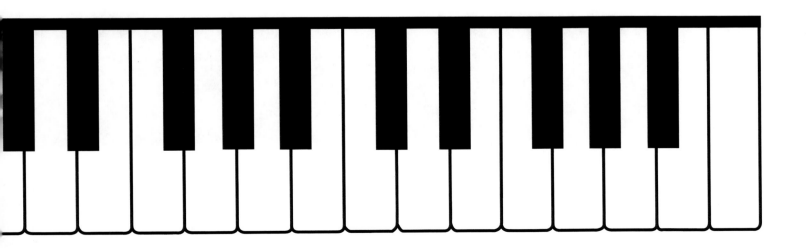

The Importance of Listening

It is important to regularly listen to good jazz in conjunction with your study and practice. *No matter how informative any book may be, it can never be a substitute for hearing this music with your own ears!* Listen often to a variety of jazz singers *and* players as part of your development in jazz singing. Below is a list of twenty specific recordings by inspirational and historically important jazz singers. If you don't already have a vocal jazz CD library established, this is a good place to start.

20 GREAT CDs!

Chet Baker
Chet Baker Sings: It Could Happen to You (Riverside)

Betty Carter
I Can't Help It (Impulse)

Nat King Cole
Cool Cole; The King Cole Trio (Proper)

Blossom Dearie
Once Upon a Summertime (Verve)

Kurt Elling
Live in Chicago (Blue Note)

Ella Fitzgerald
Ella and Basie (Verve)

Billie Holiday
Lady in Satin (Columbia)

Shirley Horn
You're My Thrill (Verve)

Eddie Jefferson
The Jazz Singer (Evidence)

Nancy King
Straight into Your Heart (Mons)

Carmen McCrae
Great American Songbook (Atlantic)

Bobby McFerrin
Bobby McFerrin (Elektra)

Mark Murphy
Rah (Original Jazz Classics)

Anita O'Day
Anita Sings the Most (Verve)

Diane Reeves
The Calling (Blue Note)

Elis Regina
Elis and Tom (Verve)

Mel Tormé
At the Red Hill/Live at the Maisonette (Collector's Choice)

Joe Williams
Everyday; The Best of the Verve Years (Verve)

Nancy Wilson
Nancy Wilson and Cannonball Adderly (Capitol)

Sarah Vaughan
How Long Has This Been Going On? (JVC)

20 SUPER Standards!

The following is a list of jazz standard songs that are in the repetoire of most professional jazz singers. If you're new to singing jazz, I recommend you use songs from this list as a starting point for establishing a repetoire for performance on *gigs*. (A *gig* is simply a professional musical performance. The term is usually associated with club or private party work rather than concerts.) These songs can be easily found through published song books or from online download services. (See Appendix III, "Professional Resouce Guide.")

1. Ain't Misbehavin'
2. All of Me
3. Angel Eyes
4. Body and Soul
5. Bye Bye Blackbird
6. Don't Get Around Much Anymore
7. Fly Me to the Moon
8. Girl from Ipanema
9. How High the Moon
10. Lullaby of Birdland
11. My Funny Valentine
12. The Nearness of You
13. Night and Day
14. One Note Samba
15. Our Love is Here To Stay
16. Route 66
17. Someone To Watch Over Me
18. Summertime
19. They Can't Take That Away From Me
20. When I Fall in Love

25 More GREAT Standards!

This list of great tunes differs from the first in that these songs are familiar but less commonly performed, making them more distinctive without being obscure. Some of these songs are more melodically or harmonically complex, yet they are all completely suitable for gigs or other performances. If you're looking for new tunes that are fairly well known yet not "super-standards," this list is a good starting point.

1. All of You
2. A Beautiful Friendship
3. Black Coffee
4. Cry Me a River
5. Desafinado
6. Devil May Care
7. Dindi
8. East of the Sun
9. Gee Baby, Ain't I Good To You
10. How Insensitive
11. How Long Has This Been Going On?
12. I Didn't Know What Time it Was
13. It Could Happen to You
14. My Foolish Heart
15. Secret Love
16. Teach Me Tonight
17. That's All
18. This Can't Be Love
19. Time After Time
20. Triste
21. When Your Lover Has Gone
22. Whisper Not
23. Willow Weep for Me
24. You Taught My Heart To Sing
25. You'd Be So Nice To Come Home To

The Artistry
chapter 1 JAZZ STANDARDS

First things first: we need songs to work with! This chapter contains *lead sheets* for five different songs which will be used as vehicles for demonstration and exercise throughout the book. (A *lead sheet* is music that is notated with melody, chord symbols, and if applicable, lyrics.) I recommend you begin by familiarizing yourself with the melody and lyrics to all songs in this chapter.

Each song has a corresponding CD track that begins with a demonstration of the melody. Immediately following is an open accompaniment so that you may practice singing the melody yourself. Also, the melody is recorded on one stereo side only so it can be turned off (via the balance knob on your stereo) when you no longer need it. Each song is played in two different keys to allow for both high and low voices to practice the songs.

I suggest you learn the songs by listening to the demonstration performances while also following along with the sheet music. Once a song is learned, it's a good idea to record yourself singing the melody to the open accompaniment portion of each given track (or by turning off the demonstration vocal), and listen back. Later, after you've worked through the first seven chapters in "The Artistry" section, I suggest you record yourself again to listen to the progress you've made.

Suggested Listening

Look for the Silver Lining
Chet Baker: *Best of Chet Baker Sings* (Pacific Jazz)
Aretha Franklin: *Sings Standards* (Sony)
Etta Jones: *From the Heart* (Original Jazz Classics)
Susannah McCorkle: *Most Requested Songs* (Concord)
Margaret Whiting: *Jerome Kern Songbook* (Verve)

Indian Summer
Tony Bennett: *Perfectly Frank* (Columbia)
Ella Fitzgerald: *Live at Newport Jazz Festival* (Legacy)
Anita O'Day: *Incomparable!* (Verve)
John Pizzarelli: *Rare Delight of You* (Telarc)
Sarah Vaughan: *Send in the Clowns* (Pablo)

The Love Nest
Nat King Cole: *Best of Nat King Cole Trio* (Blue Note)
The Hi-Lo's: *Love Nest/All Over the Place* (Collectables)

After You've Gone
Tony Bennett: *Perfectly Frank* (Columbia)
Ella Fitzgerald: *First Lady of Song* (Verve)
Shirley Horn: *Loads of Love /Shirley Horn with Horns* (Verve)
Nina Simone: *Great Nina Simone* (Empire)
Mel Tormé: *Best of the Concord Years* (Concord)

My Honey's Lovin' Arms
Kay Starr: *Jazz Singer / I Cry by Night* (Exemplar)
Ivie Anderson with Duke Ellington: *Duke's Men, Small Groups, Vol. 1* (Legacy)
Ray Nance with Duke Ellington: *It Had to Be You: A Jazz Wedding Album* (RCA Victor)
Barbara Streisand: *Barbara Streisand Album* (Columbia)

Look for the Silver Lining
(Key of Bb)

Words by B. G. DeSylva, Music by Jerome Kern
Composed in 1920

Track 1

Look for the Silver Lining
(Key of Db)

Words by B. G. DeSylva. Music by Jerome Kern
Composed in 1920

Track 2

INDIAN SUMMER
(KEY OF Eb)

Track 3

MUSIC BY VICTOR HERBERT, WORDS BY AL DUBIN
COMPOSED IN 1918

Indian Summer
(Key of G)

Track 4

Music by Victor Herbert, Words by Al Dubin
Composed in 1918

The Love Nest
(Key of C)

Words by Otto Harbach, Music by Louis A. Hirsch
Composed in 1920

Track 5

THE LOVE NEST
(KEY OF Eb)

WORDS BY OTTO HARBACH, MUSIC BY LOUIS A. HIRSCH
COMPOSED IN 1920

Track 6

After You've Gone
(Key of F)

Track 7

Words and Music by Henry Creamer and Turner Layton
Composed in 1918

B♭maj7   B♭m6   E♭7   Fmaj7   B♭9

Af - ter you've gone___ and left me cry - ing, af - ter you've gone___

Am7   D9   G7   Gm7   C7

there's no de - ny - ing, you'll feel blue,___ you'll feel sad,___

F6   F7

you'll miss the dear - est pal you've ev - er had.___

B♭maj7   B♭m6   E♭7   Fmaj7   B♭9

There'll come a time,___ now don't for - get it, there'll come a time___

Am7   D9   Gm7   D7(♭9)   Gm7   B♭m6

when you'll re - gret it, some - day when you grow lone - ly,

Fmaj7   A7   Dm7   Dm7/C   Bm7♭5   B♭7

your heart will break like mine and you'll want me on - ly.

Am7   Dm7   Gm7   C7   F

Af - ter you've gone,___ af - ter you've gone a - way___

After You've Gone
(Key of Ab)

 Track 8

Words and Music by Henry Creamer and Turner Layton
Composed in 1918

Af - ter you've gone__ and left me cry - ing, af - ter you've gone__

there's no de - ny - ing, you'll feel blue,__ you'll feel sad,__

you'll miss the dear - est pal you've ev - er had.__

There'll come a time,__ now don't for - get it, there'll come a time__

when you'll re - gret it, some - day when you grow lone - ly,

your heart will break like mine and you'll want me on - ly.

Af - ter you've gone,__ af - ter you've gone a - way__

MY HONEY'S LOVIN' ARMS
(KEY OF Eb)

Track 9

WORDS BY HERMAN RUBY, MUSIC BY JOSEPH MEYER
COMPOSED IN 1922

My Honey's Lovin' Arms
(key of G)

 Track 10

Words by Herman Ruby, Music by Joseph Meyer
Composed in 1922

chapter **2** THE NATURE OF JAZZ SINGING

Communication is the Goal

Jazz is a creative, interactive art form that requires finely tuned listening skills and a spirit of spontaneity. The ultimate goal: to communicate (specifically, to communicate emotion through the text). Great jazz performances are those where the artist has imprinted their own personal "stamp" on a song, making their rendition unique. The focus of a jazz singer's performance is more on the *singer* than on the *song* itself. While the integrity of the song is certainly an important factor, it's the artist's *interpretation* of the song that is the true essence of jazz.

Great jazz singers communicate with a sense of soulful honesty when they sing. Rather than *acting* like they feel the story of the song, they seem to really *feel* the story of the song; you believe them. Even if the setting or story line of a given song is not true for them personally, they are still able to give an honest portrayal of the *emotion* behind the scenario.

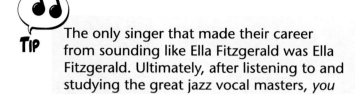

Tip The only singer that made their career from sounding like Ella Fitzgerald was Ella Fitzgerald. Ultimately, after listening to and studying the great jazz vocal masters, *you* should sound like *you*.

Jazz is a Team Sport

Rather than thinking of members of the rhythm section as your *accompanists*, it's best to consider everyone as equally important to the musical whole. Think of it like a basketball team: you've got five players (vocal, piano, bass, drums, and horn, for example), and *you're* "the forward." When you sing the melody, you're in a leadership role, and the players support you (they *pass you the ball*). However, in the end, it's the synergy of *the team* that really makes the game.

Try It!

Using any of the "20 Great CDs" from page 6 (or another of your choosing), select one track that you like and listen to it closely, twice in a row. Then write down your impressions of the song by answering the following questions:

1. Did the singer use much vibrato? _____

2. Describe the singer's vocal tone. _____

3. What was the overall mood/emotion/attitude of the performance? _____

4. Did the singer stylize much, and if so, in what ways? _____

5. What was the tempo and rhythmic groove of the song? _____

6. Did there seem to be much interaction between the singer and the players?_____

7. Did it seem that the singer had a creative interpretation of the melody
    or did they primarily sing it as written? _____

8. Explain what the text is about._____

9. What was the instrumentation of the accompaniment? _____

10. Did you "believe" the singer? Did it sound honest? _____

chapter **3** THE STORY OF THE TEXT

The primary mode of communication for a jazz singer is the meaningful delivery of the text; this is number one on the list of artistic priorities! The lyrics to a song are like a story. We want the audience to *listen* to our story and really *hear* its message.

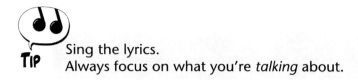

TIP Sing the lyrics.
Always focus on what you're *talking* about.

Getting Inside the Lyrics

Expressing emotion through lyrics in an effective way requires a deep understanding of the text, inside and out. Each given line of a song will fall somewhere on the communication spectrum between simple/direct, to completely metaphorical. Sometimes it's tricky to fully comprehend all of the subtleties of the lyrics; they can have hidden or dual meanings.

It can be revealing to take a close look at a song's text, line by line. Most sentences will fall into one of the following categories:

1. Informative: "I've flown around the world in a plane." (From "I Can't Get Started.")

2. Declarative: "I love your lovin' arms." (From "My Honey's Lovin' Arms.")

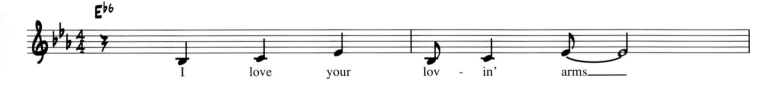

3. Inquisitive: "Skylark, have you anything to say to me?
    Won't you tell me where my love can be?" (From "Skylark.")

4. Descriptive: "Your lips were like a red and ruby chalice, warmer than the summer's night." (From "Midnight Sun.")

5. Poetic: "Glittering crowds in shimmering clouds, of canyons and steel." (From "Autumn in New York.")

6. Metaphorical: "You're the tear that comes after June time's laughter." (From "Indian Summer.")

7. Playful: "Out of the tree of life I just picked me a plum." (From "The Best is Yet to Come.")

8. Commentary: "Poor butterfly, 'neath the blossoms waiting, poor butterfly, for she loved him so." (From "Poor Butterfly.")

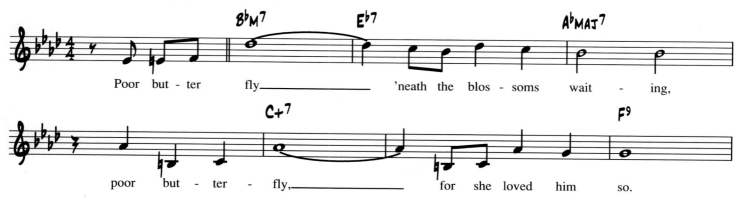

Using the following stanza from "The Love Nest" (or another song of your choosing), analyze and label each sentence using the categories above or others as necessary:

Just a love nest cozy with charm,
Like a dove nest down on a farm.
A veranda with some sort of clinging vine,
Then a kitchen where some rambler roses twine.

Another way to gain insight into the deeper meaning of the text is to examine it line by line, then paraphrase and/or explain each sentence in your own words. This process can help to uncover subtle hidden meanings and metaphors that may have been previously overlooked. Here's an example from the song, "Indian Summer:"

"Summer, you old Indian summer,"

Paraphrased: "I feel reflective; there's something special about this time of the year."

Explanation: We don't know yet what the exact scenario is; it's ambiguously reflective.

"You're the tear that comes after June-time's laughter,"

Paraphrased: "I feel sad now, and reminiscent of the joyful days of early summer."

Explanation: The Indian summer is really a metaphor for the melancholy I feel now.

"You see so many dreams that don't come true,"

Paraphrased: "The Indian Summer is full of disappointments."

Explanation: *My* dreams have not come true; I am disappointed.

"Dreams we fashioned when summertime was new."

Paraphrased: "I again reminisce about the happier times, probably with a love interest that is now gone, during the summer."

Explanation: Summer is a metaphor for joy and optimism.

Using the following stanza from "Look For the Silver Lining" (or another song of your choosing), paraphrase and/or explain each line in your own words:

Look for the Silver Lining
whene'er a cloud appears in the blue.
Remember somewhere the sun is shining,
and so the right thing to do is make it shine for you.

Personalizing the Song

Expressing a song with heartfelt honesty is possible only if you have some kind of personal connection with the lyrics. When a song's text resonates with your own experiences, there is a much better chance that you will be able to communicate in a meaningful way.

One way to bring a text "closer to home" is to create an imaginary scenario: the people involved in the story and your specific surroundings. Consider the following questions as they relate to any given song:

1. *Who are you?*
   Are you a young adult who is just starting out with enthusiasm and a fresh perspective in life? Or, a teenager who is madly in love for the first time and doesn't quite know how to handle it? Or perhaps a mature adult who has weathered some of the tough times that life has to offer?

2. *To whom are you singing?*
   Perhaps you're sitting alone thinking, or talking to yourself out loud. Or, perhaps you're confiding to a close friend, or talking face to face with the object of your love, frustration or sadness. Maybe your message is a general expression going out to the whole world, to anyone and everyone who will listen.

3. *What is the Setting?*
   Where are you right now? Perhaps you're sitting at the kitchen table at 3:00 a.m. on a sleepless night. Or, maybe you're outside gazing at the stars with the one you love. Or perhaps you're at a restaurant, or at home talking on the phone.

Try It!

Write a few sentences that describe a hypothetical scenario for the first stanza of, "After You've Gone" (or another song of your choosing). Write a total of two or three different scenarios, each one describing yourself, the setting and the people involved in the story. Then, using **CD TRACK 7 or 8**, sing the song with each of your scenarios in mind, one at a time. Notice how each has a different effect on the song's mood.

chapter **4** TEXT DELIVERY

Sing the Words as You Would Say Them

Delivering the text in a conversational way is a key factor in the effective communication of a song. In other words, your audience will hear your message when you *sing the words as you would say them.* Yes, it's true that singing a jazz tune requires more emotional intensity in the delivery of the text than would be used in everyday conversation. So, think of it this way: *sing the words as though you're a poet giving a reading of one of your favorite poems to a captive audience.* The pronunciation of the words will be conversational, yet your delivery will carry more weight of importance and at times employ artistic pauses and other expressive nuance.

Consider the relative weight of importance of each given word. In casual conversation, the *unimportant* words (grammatical words) such as "and," "the," "of," "but," "that," and "to," are typically pronounced in a way that gives them much less emphasis than the more *important* words, such as the nouns and adjectives. Let's look at an example. Say the sentence below using the vowel sounds of the words in parenthesis as your guide to the pronunciation of the preceding word:

I	went	to	the	store	but	they	were	out	of	milk	and	cheese
I	went	(do)	(huh)	store	but	they	were	out	(dove)	milk	(hand)	cheese

This is how you would normally pronounce the words in this sentence if you were speaking slowly and deliberately. However, in a faster paced, more casual conversation, the vowels would sound more like this:

I	went	to	the	store	but	they	were	out	of	milk	and	cheese
I	went	(look)	(look)	store	but	they	were	out	(look)	milk	(end)	cheese

Treating the *unimportant* words in this way will take your singing a long way toward sounding conversational. It's easy to do: simply speak the text as you would in casual conversation, then sing it exactly the same way. In cases where you sing longer, held notes for contrast or effect, revert to the less conversational pronunciation.

Using the first half of "Indian Summer" (or another song of your choosing), underline all of the *unimportant* words. Next, say each line one by one very conversationally, de-emphasizing the unimportant words, then immediately sing each line the same way.

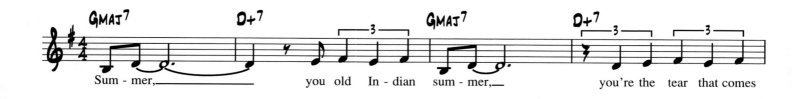

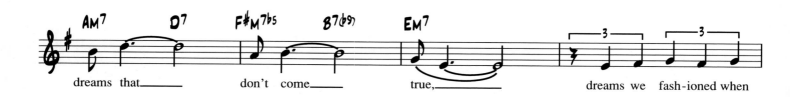

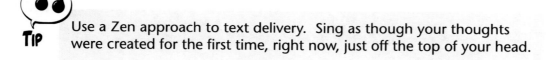

Tip   Use a Zen approach to text delivery. Sing as though your thoughts were created for the first time, right now, just off the top of your head.

Sing in Sentences

In performance (especially with ballads), it's easy to make the mistake of singing an overabundance of long, drawn-out phrases that direct too much attention to your voice and not enough to the *message of the text*. I call it "*sing-songing*," the tendency to emphasize the singing of a song without regard for making it conversational. Instead, try to adopt the habit of *singing in sentences*: make sure the meaning of each individual sentence is not obscured by too many lengthy, drawn-out phrases, whether it is a ballad or any other style. The notes you hold out when singing should be interspersed between phrases that are more speech-like. Avoid getting caught up in listening to the loveliness of your own voice; keep the focus on making sure your message is clear to the listener.

Use of Word Stress

Word stress can be a useful tool for communication in jazz singing. For example, when speaking to someone in an excited way, you *tend* to *stress* certain *words* and *syllables* to get your *point* across *strongly*. This concept transfers well to singing; it can engage the listener and help them to really *hear* your message.

One way to utilize word stress as a communicative tool is to sing each line as though you're *answering a question*. Notice in the following example of "After You've Gone" that each line of text is first put into

the form of a question, then answered in complete sentences. This automatically encourages more stress on certain syllables, giving each line a greater sense of importance:

(After you've what?) After you've *gone*

(And left me what?) And left me *cryin'*

(After who has gone?) After *you've* gone

(How much denying is there?) There's *no* denying.

Try It!

Using the first half of the lyrics from "My Honey's Lovin' Arms" (or another song of your choosing), write down each line in the form of a question, then underline the words or syllables that would naturally be stressed in the answer. (See examples in the first two lines.) Once finished, sing this entire passage along with **CD TRACK 9 or 10**.

QUESTION: How do I feel about your lovin' arms?

ANSWER: I *love* your lovin' arms.

QUESTION: What do they hold?

ANSWER: They hold a *world of charms*.

QUESTION: _____

ANSWER: A place to nestle when I am lonely.

QUESTION: _____

ANSWER: A cozy Morris chair.

QUESTION: _____

ANSWER: Oh what a happy pair.

QUESTION: _____

ANSWER: One caress, happiness, seems to bless my little honey.

Creating an Emotional Mood

Have you ever been so completely enraptured by a live performance that you forgot that anything else existed outside the room at that moment? The ability for an artist to have an entire audience completely wrapped up in the mood of the moment makes for very powerful performances!

Establishing a strong sense of performance mood begins with having a good awareness of the emotion underlying a song's text. Lyrics can usually be interpreted from several different emotional perspectives. For example, take a look at the following lines from "After You've Gone:"

> *After you've gone, and left me crying*
> *After you've gone, there's no denying*
> *You'll feel blue, you'll feel sad*
> *You'll miss the dearest pal you've ever had.*

Clearly, this is not a happy lyric. But, what type of *unhappy* is it? For example, this text could be performed with casual nonchalance (along with an underlying implication of false apathy), as if suggesting that "you didn't care that much." To convey this matter-of-fact attitude, you would avoid strong word stresses, use minimal ornamentation, and the vocal tone would be "middle of the road." In short, you would do nothing to call special attention to the song. Or, the same text could be interpreted in a sad way by using a richer vocal tone and vocal inflection, giving it more emotional depth. Or, the song could be portrayed with a bitter attitude by the use of shorter, more abrupt phrases, a more biting tone and very deliberate word stresses.

Listen

 Track 11

For any song you plan to perform, consider the lyrics in terms of what type of emotional climate(s) you want to create: introspective, joyful, irritated, secretive, silly, flamboyant, bluesy, carefree, intimate, melancholy, frustrated, playful, reflective, and so on. The moods can shift around within the song in accordance with the twists and turns of the story line. Listen to any great jazz singer such as Nancy Wilson or Mark Murphy, and notice that in each and every line they sing, you hear a clear emotional mood.

 Try It!

Using the first half of "Look For the Silver Lining" (or another song of your choosing), list three different emotional moods that could be conveyed. For example, joyful/extroverted, reflective and playful. Then sing the passage three times with **CD TRACK 1 or 2**, altering the melody, ornamenting, and stylizing as necessary to reflect each of the three different moods.

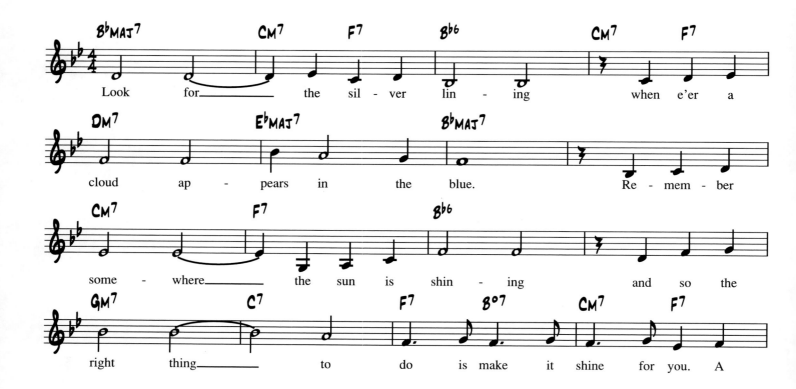

chapter 5 COLORING THE MELODY

Stylistic Tools

The way a jazz singer *stylizes* (using performance elements such as vibrato, tone color and inflection), is a primary feature of their individual *sound*. Such stylistic elements are like a playground of musical toys available to jazz singers; they help shape and mold the flavor of the music. Here are a few commonly used stylistic tools:

Listen

 Track 12

1. Vibrato

Vibrato is used in jazz as an element of stylistic choice; in other words, it doesn't necessarily have to be present all the time. Vibrato may be minimal or prolific, fast or slow, narrow or wide, depending on the personal style of the individual and the particular song. A jazz singer might use vibrato on some notes and not on others, reserve it for the end of held notes only, or sing with a straight tone completely at times.

2. Tone Color

Most jazz singers exploit the different possible timbres of their voice to help express emotion. Vocal tone colors may vary from rich and warm, to bright and focused, to breathy, and everything in between.

3. Dynamic Contrasts

Don't forget about the possibility of using simple contrasts of loud and soft to help create interest and express emotion. Dynamic changes can be slow and occur over a long period of time, or they can be sudden and dramatic.

Tip Jazz singers often begin long-held notes with a straight tone, then allow the vibrato to come in midway through the note. This is a key difference between jazz and most classical and musical theater styles.

4. Inflection

Inflection is the slight bending of a note up or down to another note. Virtually all jazz singers use inflection to some extent and, in many cases, the use of inflection is prolific.

Sum - mer,___ you old___ In - dian sum - mer___

5. Ornamentation

Ornamentation is the decoration of a note with a series of inflections, or by surrounding the note, melodically.

Sum - mer,___ you old___ In - dian sum - mer___

Try It! Using the first two lines of "The Love Nest" (or another song of your choosing), apply each of the stylistic tools outlined above, one at a time. It is likely that you'll find that you're comfortable with some more than with others; this will be your guide on how to best spend practice time! Then, choose another song from Chapter One, and sing it along with its corresponding CD track while freely experimenting with various stylistic elements. As always, it's very helpful to record yourself and listen back.

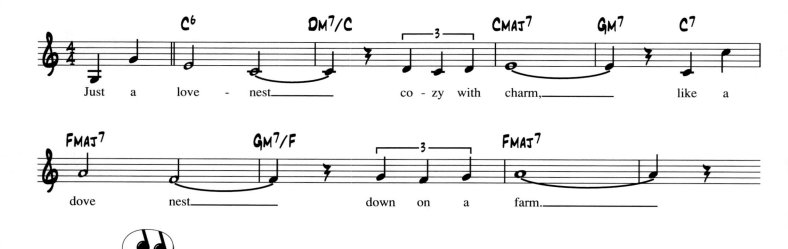

Tip Don't overindulge in the use of stylistic elements. Keep your eye on the ball: the communication of the text and the emotion behind it. All elements of style should serve the text.

The Melodic Canvas

Some jazz singers stay close to the original melody when performing while others stray so far from it that the original song is hardly recognizable. Who's to say which way is better or more appropriate? One point of view would argue that the integrity of the song must be retained to honor the composer, while the other point of view would argue that high levels of creativity are an inherent feature of any jazz performance.

When relating this issue to great masters of painting, it would seem absurd, for example, to criticize Picasso for depicting faces that didn't look "normal," or to complain that Rembrandt's work was too "predictable." With this in mind, it seems clear that

the degree to which a singer "rewrites" the melody boils down to a matter of personal artistic choice. Most jazz singers do make melodic and rhythmic alterations in the songs they sing, but the extent to which they do so varies with each individual artist.

Techniques for Melodic Variation

Below are specific methods for making creative melodic alterations. The first line of "Look for the Silver Lining" is used as an example. Keep in mind, there are virtually limitless choices to approaching a song creatively; it's possible to sing and resing a melodic phrase dozens of different ways.

Tip It is often said that in jazz, "*there are no mistakes!*" Get comfortable with this idea. The spirit of improvisation and musical adventure outweighs the quest for perfection.

Original Melody

1. Neighbor Notes

Look___ for___   the   sil - ver   lin - ing___

2. Passing Notes

Look   for   the___ sil - ver   lin - ing___

3. Chromatic-Approach Notes

Look___ for___   the   sil - ver   lin - ing___

4. Arpeggiated Melodic Lines

Look___ for___   the   sil - ver   lin - ing___

5. Melodic Leaps

Look   for_____   the sil - ver   lin - ing___

6. Change of Direction

Look   for   the   sil - ver   lin - ing___

7. Octave Displacement

Look   for_____ the   sil - ver   lin - ing___

8. Simplification

Look for   the sil - ver lin - ing

9. Melisma

Look for_____ the sil - ver lin - ing___

TIP Melisma is used in jazz in a different way than it would be in the music of Handle, or Aretha Franklin! Melisma is the singing of various notes on a single syllable or word. (Sarah Vaughan used melisma extensively in her singing.)

Try It! Using the first two lines from "After You've Gone" (or another song of your choosing), apply each of the techniques for melodic variation, one at a time. You may find it helpful to write down your melodic choices to see how they work against the original. Then, sing another of the songs from Chapter One along with its corresponding **CD TRACK**, and freely experiment with various elements of melodic variation. As always, it is very helpful to record yourself and listen back.

Af - ter you've gone_   and left me cry-ing,   af - ter you've gone_   there's no de - ny-ing,

Small Changes Go a Long Way

I find that singers who are new to jazz tend to go overboard in their initial attempts at making creative melodic changes; they try to do too much. It's often the case that very simple melodic alterations are the most musical. A few note changes here and there can add just enough interest to enhance the text and engage the listener. The bottom line is this: *any note changes must serve the "big picture" goal of honest communication of emotion through text.* For this reason, note changes should be meaningful, *serving the text rather than detracting from it.*

chapter **6** PHRASING IS YOUR FRIEND!

Phrasing is perhaps the single most important creative tool at a jazz singer's disposal! Regardless of the amount of stylization and melodic variation used, without a creative approach to *phrasing*, a singer will never sound like a jazz singer.

Phrasing Basics

Most jazz standard songs are written in a predictable, repetitive phrase structure. Consider for example, "Autumn Leaves." Each 2-measure melodic line during the first 16 bars begins and ends on the same beat of the measure, and has almost exactly the same rhythm:

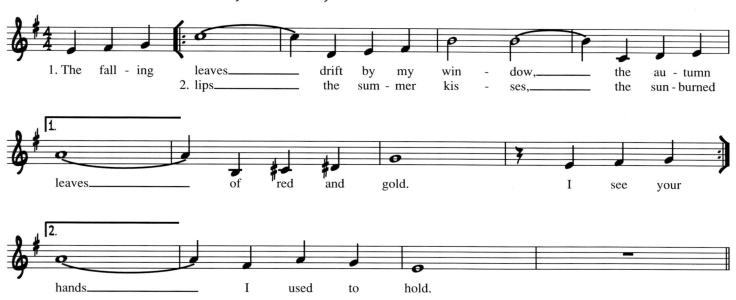

Back Phrasing

A creative approach to phrasing in this song will involve starting some of the phrases earlier or later than originally written. *Back phrasing* is the process of delaying the start of a phrase by a couple of beats or more from its original starting point. This phrasing concept is extremely common in jazz singing, and it helps to serve the goal of singing conversationally since it usually results in the words being placed closer together. Take a look at the following example of back phrasing in "Autumn Leaves:"

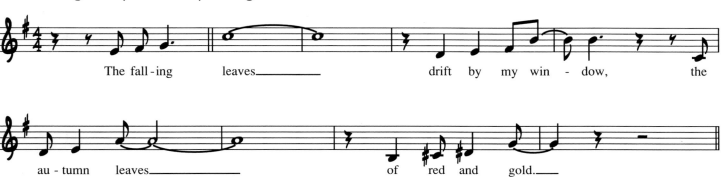

Forward Phrasing

Less common, but still very useful, is *forward phrasing*. In forward phrasing, phrases begin at an earlier starting point than originally written. Forward phrasing is common among Brazilian singers such as Astrid Gilberto and Elis Regina, but can be used in any jazz style:

To have confidence in your ability to "play" with the phrasing of a song, you must first have a strong internal confidence about where the *original* phrases of the song were in relationship to the chord progression. Once your inner awareness of the original phrase structure is solid, you can then change the phrasing to your heart's desire without losing your place in the song.

Phrasing Over the Bar Line

Phrasing over the bar line refers to the suspension of a phrase or phrases over the predictable 2-, 4-, or 8-bar divisions of a song's original phrase structure. Phrasing over the bar line is often a natural result of using back or forward phrasing. Other ways to phrase over the bar-line include holding a note longer than expected, or connecting phrases that normally have a breath in between.

The best recipe for success is to use a *combination* of phrasing choices that help to express the text in a creative way. Listen to the recorded examples of back phrasing, forward phrasing, and phrasing over the bar line as applied to "Look for the Silver Lining," on **CD TRACK 14**.

Listen

Track 14

Using "My Honey's Lovin' Arms" (or another song of your choosing), experiment with back phrasing, forward phrasing, and phrasing over the bar line while singing with the recorded accompaniment on **CD TRACK 9 or 10**.

The Power of Space

Phrasing in a creative way naturally lends itself to making creative use of space. Jazz singers often use the blank spaces between phrases as a part of their arsenal of expressive tools; space can have a powerful effect. For example, the intensity of a slightly prolonged blank space after a phrase will create a sense of anticipation, giving much more meaningful importance to the phrase coming after it. Think of open spaces as "pregnant pauses" rather than empty voids in the music. Nancy Wilson and Shirley Horn are both masters of the powerful use of space.

Listen

 Track 15

TIP Don't let too much time go by in a song without some element of surprise. The surprise can be in the phrasing, note alterations, dynamics, style, or any number of things. Work for a balance between predictability and surprise.

Breathing Matters

The breath taken before the start of any given phrase should reflect the mood of that phrase. In other words, the flavor of a phrase begins with the character of the breath attached to it. A long and relaxed phrase should be preceded by an easy, relaxed breath, and so on. Any mismatch between the character of the breath and the phrase it's attached to may distract the listener and break the mood.

Ideally, taking breaths that match the spirit of their corresponding phrases will happen naturally, though I find that for some singers, it does not. For this reason, using a recorder during practice is highly recommended. Avoid the tendency to end each phrase with an immediate in-take of breath going into the next phrase; the listener needs occasional moments of silence to "rest" and "digest."

TIP Take your breaths in any of the same places you would take them when reciting an artful poem. Rule of thumb: if the breath sounds awkward when speaking, it will sound awkward when singing.

Rubato

Rubato simply means, no tempo. (You can't dance to it!) Usually there is only a single accompaniment instrument in rubato: piano or guitar. An entire song can be performed rubato, but it is most often used for either the verse of a song (see *Song Form*, Chapter 8), or the first eight or 16 bars of a tune, before going into tempo.

Rubato is very elastic by nature, with the accompanist speeding up and slowing down to mirror the singer's speech-like style of singing. Think of rubato like *talking on pitch*, with periodic held notes. When the verse of a jazz standard is sung rubato, it's analogous to the recitative in an aria: a speech-like introduction which sets up the story line of the main body of the song.

Then there's the question of who leads during a rubato passage, the *singer* or the *accompanist*? This is a difficult question to answer because in a jazz setting, the two musicians are *interactive*; listening to each other, breathing with each other, making spontaneous pacing and dynamic changes together, and so on. Though the singer must be in more of a leadership role because he or she is the one carrying the melody, it should generally be thought of as an interactive process: a team effort.

Listen

 Track 16

TIP The term *phrasing* is also used to describe the manner in which the text is delivered, in terms of the conversational quality and use of word stress.

chapter 7 IT DON'T MEAN A THING IF...

. . . it ain't got that *swing*. Perhaps you've heard that somewhere before! Swing feel is fundamental to jazz. The best way to work on your swing feel is to listen to singers and players who are swinging! You'll find that there are numerous rhythmic patterns that are used over and over again. Through repeated listening, the rhythmic *language* of swing will sink into your ear naturally.

The ABCs of Swing

In swing feel there is an underlying steady current of *swing eighths* that must be felt internally, *all* the time (*swing eighths* are eighth notes that are interpreted as a triplet with the first two notes tied):

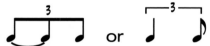

This inner feeling of triplets is a fundamental aspect of swing feel. If you're new to swing feel, try it by saying the following line in a steady tempo, with emphasis on the syllable "let":

Now, do the same with the following words, still emphasizing the third word of each triplet:

Finally, say the following with the same underlying rhythmic feeling (this will require you to elongate the word "one"):

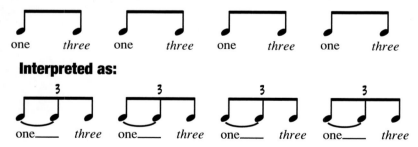

You have just spoken (swung!) a measure of swing eighth notes. Note that the *second* note of each pair of eighth notes is stressed, creating *off-beat syncopation*: tri-*plet*, tri-*plet*. Coordinating these off-beat accents with regularity can be a little awkward at first, yet it's an important part of the equation. If swing feel is new for you, it will probably take some practice before becoming automatic. It might be helpful to think about a feeling of jumping up on the off beats, and sitting down on the downbeats.

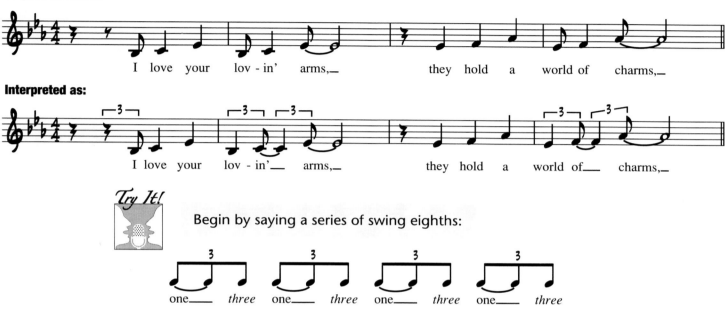

Another fundamental aspect of swing feel is an underlying feeling of accent on beats two and four. This is why we snap on beats two and four rather than one and three when in swing feel.

In written music where swing feel is designated, eighth notes will always be interpreted as swing eighth notes. Here's an example of one line of a song, first written in normal eighth-note notation, then written *as it should be interpreted* in a swing feel:

Original notation:

I love your lov - in' arms,— they hold a world of charms,—

Interpreted as:

I love your lov - in'— arms,— they hold a world of— charms,—

Try It!

Begin by saying a series of swing eighths:

one— three one— three one— three one— three

Once you're comfortable with the natural lilt of the swing feel, sing the first half of "After You've Gone" (or another song of your choosing) with **CD TRACK 7 or 8** while retaining the same underlying rhythmic feeling. Continue singing the song, and referring back to the "one-three, one-three," chant as a reminder of the inner rhythm as necessary.

Take your breaths in tempo when in swing feel. If the breath is not in tempo, you'll have difficulty swinging the phrase.

Laying Back

Once the inner rhythm of swing eighth notes is strongly internalized, the next step in developing a good swing feel is to *lay back*. (*Laying back* is the placement of rhythms very slightly behind each steady quarter-note beat.) In swing feel at medium and slow tempos, there is virtually always some amount of laying back. The subtle difference between singing exactly on the beat and slightly behind it makes all the difference in the world in terms of *grooving*. (To *groove* is to sing or play with a good rhythmic feel.)

Listen

Track 17

Don't lose your sense of energy and vitality when laying back. The two can (and should) coexist!

A song's tempo can have a great effect on how you handle the song, rhythmically. For example, in a fast tempo, you can't lay back very far or the song will leave you in the dust before you know it! Fast tunes require that you sing more on the front side of the beat with a sense of command, as if you're driving the car rather than being a passenger.

The opposite is true for slow swing tunes where you have the opportunity to dig in deeply to the swing feel and lay back a great deal. It can feel like there's an eternity between each beat on a slow swinging tune, allowing plenty of time to stylize and ornament.

Try It!

Sing "My Honey's Lovin' Arms" (or another song of your choosing) along with **CD Track 9 or 10**, first singing directly on the steady beat, then laying back. Experiment with various degrees of laying back.

Tip Patience is a virtue in swing feel. Especially on medium and slower tempos, don't be in a hurry, or it won't swing!

Rhythmic Choices

Jazz singers typically bring a creative approach to the rhythms of a song, just as they do for melody, style and phrasing. Many of the tunes that are performed as swing tunes were *originally* written as ballads, full of whole, half and quarter notes. Sung as written, these songs have absolutely no hope of swinging because of the absence of eighth notes. The rhythms must be rewritten in these cases to integrate eighth notes. This will allow the triplet eighth-note feeling (which is so fundamental to swing feel) to be present. Take a look at the first eight bars of "Autumn Leaves:"

You can see that this example contains only quarter, half and whole notes. This is the way the tune was originally written. To interpret this song in a swing style, the rhythms will need the incorporation of a few eighth notes, strategically devised to create off-beat syncopation in the *anticipation* or *delay* of a beat:

Notice that the off-beat syncopation created in the example above naturally coincides with the undercurrent of off-beat accents characteristic of swing feel. You'll find that there is a prolific use of eighth-note off-beat accents in swing music.

Tip All rhythmic styles (including swing, Latin styles, rock styles, and so on) are felt and performed in *relationship* to the steady beat. Some styles tend to be felt a little more *on top* (on the front side) of the beat, and others are felt slightly behind (on the back side) of the steady beat. For this reason, it's important to develop a strong sense of steady beat by practicing with a metronome!

Usually, there are several workable rhythmic choices for any one phrase.
Here are three examples of "My Honey's Lovin' Arms," each with different rhythms:

Listen

Track 18

Example 1:

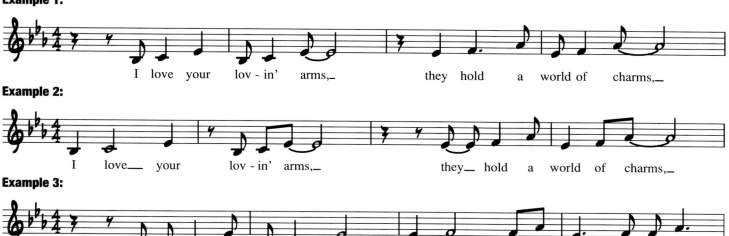

Example 2:

Example 3:

Despite the rhythmic activity of the example above, the text will still sound conversationally natural when sung. This is because *the rhythms have been devised to work in cooperation with the natural word stresses in the text.* If in doubt about whether a swing rhythm works well for a given line of text, try talking it in tempo. It will become immediately apparent whether or not your rhythmic choices are compatible with the lyrics. Sometimes, finding workable rhythms takes experimentation.

Try It!

Using "After You've Gone" (or another song of your choosing), write out the first eight measures four times, each with different rhythms. Experiment with your options by speaking the lines in rhythm until you find choices that allow the text to sound natural. Then sing each line either a cappella or with **CD TRACK 7 or 8.**

TIP
Another useful rhythmic concept is what I call *"preach-singing"*: the periodic interjection of phrases that are extraordinarily talkative in spirit and completely *out of the groove,* reminiscent of a preacher giving a passionate sermon. Carmen McCrae used this device as a regular part of her style. Think of it like talking on pitch, enthusiastically.

Listen
Track 19

Are You "Rhythmically Challenged?"

Try the following remedies:

1. Walk in Tempo

Walk around the room in tempo with your feet stepping in quarter notes while you sing a song.

2. Move Your Arm in Rhythmic Circles

Rotate your arm in the air as though you're beckoning someone to come near to you. Your arm should rotate a full circle for each quarter-note beat, and it should reflect the feeling of swing eighth notes. (Think of how a raw egg would lope along when rolled across a table.)

3. Tap While Singing

Turn on a metronome and sing while you simultaneously tap your leg in quarter notes to the beat. Once comfortable, tap every other quarter note on beats two and four. Until you can tap while singing, you won't be able to swing!

4. Talk the Song in Tempo

By speaking the text of a song in swing feel, you can freely experiment with rhythmic choices without having to deal with melodic or vocal issues.

5. Converse in Rhythm

Have a conversation with someone, or read out of a book, talk to yourself about the meaning of life, or whatever, but do it in *swing feel* (with an underlying feeling of swing eighth notes.) The idea is for the swing feel to become second nature to you.

6. Sing With a Recording

Choose a swinging recording and sing along with it, trying to match all the subtleties of rhythmic feel and other nuances as exactly as possible.

Try It!

Sing "My Honey's Lovin' Arms" (or another song of your choosing) along with **CD TRACK 20**. This track contains only drums and a voice counting out the beats of each measure. Practicing with this track will help you learn to keep track of where beat one is at all times!

Congratulations on the progress you've made in working through the first seven chapters. You should be well on your way to singing jazz with style, artistry and creative expression.

The next group of chapters will help you round out your musicianship skills and understanding of jazz concepts such as rhythmic styles, lead-sheet writing, communicating with rhythm section players, and so on. Your expertise in these areas will give you the foundation to sing jazz with complete confidence and to operate as a professional.

chapter **8** Preparing to Sing a New Tune

Choose a Song

It should not be difficult to find a tune you like and are inspired to sing; there are numerous great tunes available through recordings or *fake books*. (A *fake book* is a compilation of tunes notated with melody and chord symbols only.) Many songs that are not normally considered *jazz standards*, such as pop and Broadway show tunes, can often be adapted to fit well into a jazz setting. (A *jazz standard* is a song that is in the repertoire of most professional jazz musicians because it is so well known and commonly performed. Most of the tunes considered to be jazz standards were written prior to the 1960s.) Almost any song is potentially fair game as long as it can be *interpreted* in a jazz style, though you may have to make adjustments in the chord progression.

Check the tune you are considering for built-in challenges like extremities of range, difficult melodic passages, or tricky rhythms. Also, look closely at the message of the text to see if it's something you're inspired to sing. Many of the standards have lyrics that are dated, and may even seem a little *corny* by today's standards, but if you can relate to the underlying *sentiment* of the tune, then it may still be a good vehicle for you.

Learn the Original Melody

Be sure to learn the *original* written melody of the song. Since most jazz singers take significant liberties with any song they sing, their recordings are not reliable sources for learning the correct melody. It's important for purposes of musical integrity and respect for the tune's composer to learn the song correctly, not just Mel Torme's or Diane Reeves's version. This step will probably require you to use the piano.

Tip Learn *style* from listening to other singers and players.
Learn the *song* from the written music.

Determine the Song Form

The organizational structure of a song is referred to as its *song form*. Virtually all jazz standard songs are written in 8-, 10- or 12-measure sections, some of which repeat one or more times in the tune. In performance, you need to be aware of the song form to keep track of where you are in the song. Particularly during instrumental solos, it's easy to get lost unless you're following the song form in your mind!

The bulk of the jazz standards are in *AABA* form or *ABAC* (or its close variation, *ABAB*). Each section is normally eight measures long, adding up to a total of 32 bars for the full song. (*Bar* is another term for *measure*.) Common AABA tunes include "My Funny Valentine," "Ain't Misbehavin'" and "Night and Day."

A	**A**	**B**	**A**
8 MEASURES	REPEAT 1ST 8 MEASURES	8 NEW MEASURES	REPEAT 1ST 8 MEASURES

Common ABAC (or ABAB) tunes include "All of Me," "Fly me To the Moon," and "When I Fall in Love."

A	**B**	**A**	**C**
8 MEASURES	8 NEW MEASURES	REPEAT 1ST 8 MEASURES	8 NEW MEASURES

The B section of an AABA tune is referred to as *the bridge*, and the middle of an ABAC (or ABAB) tune is commonly referred to as *the second half.* Using this type of terminology will help you communicate effectively with other musicians, with jargon such as, "You take a solo at the top and then I'll come back in on the second half." Or, "After the first *chorus*, let's go directly back to the bridge and take it out from there." (A *chorus* is one complete time through the song form.)

It is not uncommon to find variations in the above song form prototypes. For example, "A Foggy Day" is basically ABAC, but has a 10-bar C section. "Alone Together" is basically AABA, but the first two A sections are each 14 measures rather than the usual eight. "Gee Baby Ain't I Good to You" is clearly

AABA, but each of the four sections are only four bars long. "Autumn Leaves" is very similar to an AABA type tune, but the last A section is different than the others, making it an AABC form. Occasionally you'll find songs that simply have their own unique song form.

Jazz standard tunes will sometimes have a *verse*. The verse, as it is considered in the context of jazz standard song forms, is an introductory passage occurring before the main body of the song. It is usually performed rubato. Most tunes with verses come from Broadway shows. The beginning of the well-known tune, "Someone To Watch Over Me" is a classic example of a verse. Several of the songs from Chapter One have a verse, for example, here is the verse from "Look for the Silver Lining":

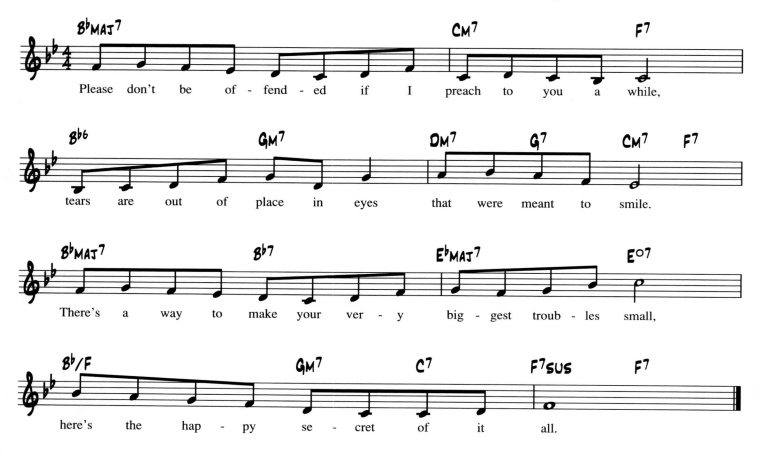

Many jazz standard songs such as this one *have* a verse which is not customarily performed. It's probably the case that many singers are not even aware that a verse *exists* for such tunes as "I Left My Heart in San Francisco," and "It Had to Be You." Please know that the Sher Music "Standards Real Book" fake book *does* include the verse for any tune that has one. This is a nice feature!

To determine the song form of a tune, start at the beginning (*after* the verse if there is one), and count measures. After the first eight bars, if the melody and chords generally stay the same, there's a high likelihood that it's an AABA tune. Then examine the rest of the tune to the end, looking for similarities and differences between sections to determine the song's form. If after the first eight bars you find that the melody and chord changes differ, then it's likely that the song form is ABAC or its variation, ABAB.

Try It!

Using "Indian Summer" (or another song of your choosing), analyze the song form by following the guideline above. Simply write in the letters A, B or C as appropriate above the first measure where each new section begins. (See the lead sheet for "Indian Summer," Chapter 1.)

Twelve-bar blues is both a song form and chord progression. It is an important part of the historical roots of both jazz and rock genres, and is still commonly heard in both styles. The chord progression of 12-bar blues can vary a great deal depending on the musical context. For example, here is a very basic, bare-bones blues progression:

F⁷ | F⁷ | F⁷ | F⁷ | B♭⁷ | B♭⁷ | F⁷ | F⁷ | C⁷ | B♭⁷ | F⁷ | C⁷ ‖

Here is another example of a blues progression, the way jazz musicians might play it. Notice that although this progression is very different from the one above, the *first*, *fifth* and *eleventh* measures contain the same chord in both examples:

F⁷ | B♭⁷ | F⁷ | CM⁷ F⁷ | B♭⁷ | B°⁷ | F⁷/C | D⁷ | GM⁷ | C⁷ | F⁷ | GM⁷ C⁷ ‖

Blues tunes used in jazz include "Route 66," "Centerpiece," "Red Top," "Twisted," and numerous others. Remember that many 12-bar blues tunes appear much longer than 12 measures because there are multiple verses of the text, such as in "Route 66." (The term *verses* is used here in the traditional sense.) Songs written in a 12-bar blues form should not be confused with 32-bar tunes that happen to be *bluesy* in character, such as "Since I Fell for You."

Choose the Key

Determine the key for the song that best suits your voice (see Chapter 9, "Transposing"), with consideration for what keys are appropriate in a jazz setting.

In preparation for writing this book, I asked numerous singers and players about what they consider to be appropriate keys to use for jazz standards on the average gig. The diversity in the feedback I got was substantial! There seems to be two main schools of thought: the first is that any key is OK if it's the best one for the singer, and the second is that certain keys should be avoided because they are not traditionally used in jazz settings and/or don't lay well on certain *axes*. (*Axe* is a slang term for instrument.) While it's true that experienced players *can* play well in any key, they probably have played in *some* keys much more frequently than others. Glance through any jazz fake book and you'll see that most of the standard tunes

are written in C, F, B♭, E♭, A♭ or G. Instrumentalists tend to play songs in their original key, so it's easy to see why this group of key centers would become quite comfortable for most players.

Here's my thought on the question of appropriate keys, based on my background as both pianist and singer and on the feedback I got from others: the most universally accepted keys for playing jazz standards are C, F, B♭, E♭, A♭ and G. These keys are comfortable for most players; they are *safe* for virtually any situation. The keys of D♭ and D are a bit more controversial. Personally, as a pianist I like playing in D♭, but I am not as comfortable playing standards in D. Other players, however, feel the opposite way. It's generally not a good idea to call tunes in a key with more than two sharps (A, E, B, F♯) unless you are sure the players will be comfortable with it. If in doubt about the comfort zone and sentiments of whom you're working with, it's best to play it safe.

TIP Remember that the key that feels comfortable when you're at home and relaxed may be *too low* when you're in performance and trying to be heard over a rhythm section.

Decide the Rhythmic Feel and Tempo

As a jazz artist, it's fair-game to take any tune and perform it in any rhythmic style. There's no rule that says a certain song must be performed as a ballad just because it's normally done that way. This is part of the fun of jazz. "When I Fall in Love" for example, which is traditionally performed as a ballad, could work well as a bright swing tune. "They Can't Take That Away From Me," which is traditionally swing, could be turned into a ballad. "Fly Me to the Moon" could work as a samba. Don't hesitate to be creative with your rhythmic feel and tempo choices. (Refer to Chapter 13, "Rhythmic Grooves and Playing Styles.")

Listen to Recordings of the Tune

There is no educational substitute for listening to jazz music! Find a recording of a vocalist singing your chosen song, or a song that's very similar, and listen to how they handle the phrasing, style, note changes, rhythmic feel, mood/attitude, and so on. The more jazz singers you've listened to closely, the greater a repertoire of ideas you will have for developing your *own* style.

Practice

It's very helpful to use a recorded accompaniment when you practice your jazz singing. There are several computer programs available, such as *Band in a Box*, and *Smart Music Studio*, expressly for this purpose. Recorded accompaniments featuring live players are available from most major publishers, such as the *Jamey Aebersold* series or the *Alfred MasterTracks* series. Or, you can have a pianist or guitarist record an accompaniment for you. And best yet, if you have the piano or guitar skills, record your own accompaniment!

The first priority in practicing should be to learn the song well, and to work out any quirks, such as passages that are vocally challenging or melodic lines that are hard to hear. Then, experiment with creative note, rhythm and phrasing alterations. The more you stretch yourself in practice to find different ways of interpreting a song, the more creative flexibility and confidence you'll have in performance.

It's always a good idea to record yourself and listen back as a regular part of your practice. You will learn more from listening to a recording of yourself than any amount of feedback from another person or info from a book. It is also strongly recommended that you use a metronome in the practice of swing and other tunes in rhythm. Development of a strong sense of internal steady time is vital to swing feel and other rhythmic grooves. Simply turn on the metronome and sing as if it were an accompaniment. You could have the metronome click on all four beats, or if in swing feel, beats two and four only.

Tip

You will get better if you practice.
You probably won't get much better if you don't.
What a concept!

chapter **9** WRITING A LEAD SHEET

Lead-Sheet Styles

A lead sheet is music that is notated with melody, chord symbols and if applicable, lyrics. With the exception of big bands, jazz musicians rarely (if ever) use scores that are written out note for note; lead sheets are the norm. There are two styles of lead sheets. **Lead Sheet Style 1** is by far the most common, and uses a single-stave format:

Rhythm section players are more concerned with the chord changes of a song than the melody and lyrics, and for that reason lead sheets are often written with only chord symbols and *slashes* that represent beats of the measure:

This type of lead sheet is quite common and sufficient for use on most gigs, simple as it may be. The entire gig book of many jazz singers is made up of lead sheets with chord symbols and slashes only.

Tip With less experienced players, it's a good idea to include the melody on your lead sheets. This may help them play for you in a more musical way because they can visually follow along with your singing, making it easier to complement you. It also allows them the possibility of being able to reference the melody in their intros or other places in the song.

Lead Sheet Style 2 represents the music in a double-stave format, allowing the melody and lyrics to be especially clear and easy to read:

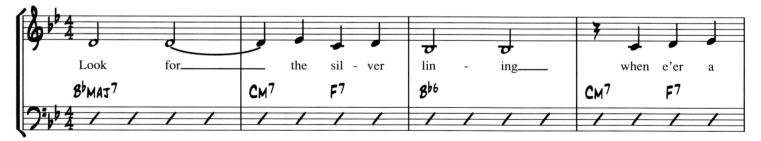

Lead Sheet Style 2 is useful in situations when the pianist needs to closely follow the singer, such as in rubato. It is also commonly used when a written out piano or bass part is required.

Basic Layout

The goal is for your lead sheet to be as clear and legible as possible, making it easy to read. We'll use a single-stave lead sheet with slashes as an example.

1. **Write in the title and composer at the top, the rhythmic style (swing or bossa for example) on the left side, the key signature and the time signature on the first stave.** Optional: write in a specific tempo marking.

2. **Determine the song form of the tune and mark in all bar lines accordingly.** Optional: leave the top line open for the addition of an intro later. Use a ruler when marking bar lines, and try to make four measure lines in most cases. Use repeats when possible rather than writing out the entire tune long hand. (See Chapter 8 for more about song form.)

Tip Pickup notes (such as first three notes of "Autumn Leaves") would be sung during the final bar of the intro; *don't add an extra measure in the intro* to accommodate them. *Pickups* are melodic notes that occur before the first complete measure of a phrase.

Example Lead Sheet 1, "Lullaby of Birdland," shows the layout of a typical AABA tune. Notice that there are six measures on the second line to accommodate slight differences between the first and second A sections.

Example Lead Sheet 2, "When I Fall in Love," shows the typical layout of an ABAC tune. Notice that repeat markings with long first and second endings are used to accommodate the B and C sections of the tune.

In both lead-sheet examples, the key signature is written on each line as a reminder. This is optional for lead sheets that have slashes and chord symbols only, though it's recommended for lead sheets that have the melody written. The clef is only necessary for the top staff. The others may have the key signature only. Notice also the placement of double bar lines throughout the lead sheet which give a clear visual indication of the dividing lines between primary sections. These double bars help to organize the lead sheet and make it easier to read. Make every effort to start each section on the far left or exact middle of the page to reflect the structure and symmetry of the song.

TIP Think even numbers: intros are USUALLY four or eight bars, A and B sections are eight, or occasionally 10 or 12. You would virtually *never* see a five bar intro, or seven-bar A section!

3. **Write in the chord symbols above each measure and slashes on the stave.** Slashes should be tilted at a slight angle, and placed on the three inner lines of the stave. Take care to place the chord symbol exactly above the beat of the measure where the chord is to be played. You can use the repeat symbol (℀) to indicate a repetition of the chord(s) in the previous measure.

You should write in the melody and words if the song is not well known, or in cases where the players have to follow you closely, such as in rubato. (Some singers prefer to write in melody and words on all of their lead sheets. It boils down to a matter of personal preference, and the experience level of the players with whom you'll be working.) When writing in the melody and words, you may not be able to retain the symmetrical four measures per line because of the extra space required by the text. Plan for as many measures per line as needed to be sure the lyrics are clearly readable, and again, try when possible to start each new section on the far left or exact middle of the page.

TIP It is not necessary to put rehearsal letters on most short, basic lead sheets.

Write It!

Use a song of your choosing from a published fake book and write a single stave, chords and slashes only lead sheet for it.

Transposing

Often a song will need to be *transposed* to best suit your vocal range. (*Transposing* is the changing of a song's key from one to another.) Be sure to choose a key that's appropriate in a jazz context. (See page 43) Follow this step-by-step process:

TIP There are numerous good computer programs available for lead-sheet writing. However, whether or not you use a program to save time, it's still necessary to have a working knowledge of the information presented in this chapter.

1. Determine the original key of the song.

Don't forget that any given key signature can actually represent one of two different keys: a certain major key, *OR* its relative minor. For example, E-flat major and C minor share the same key signature. Also, be aware that the first chord of the song is *not* a reliable factor in determining the key. It's the *final* chord of the song that most conclusively represents the song's key. (For example "After You've Gone" from Chapter 1 begins in the key of B-flat major but ends in the key of F major. The overall key is F major.)

2. Find the key that best suits your vocal range.

Search for the highest and lowest melodic notes in the song. Then go to the piano, play these two notes simultaneously, and consider how they relate to your comfortable singing range.

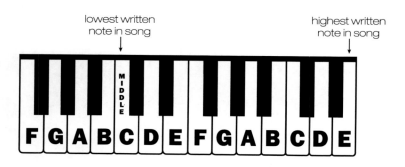

If one of the two notes seems too high or low, then at the piano, walk them both up or down in parallel half-step increments until they *both* lay in your comfortable range.

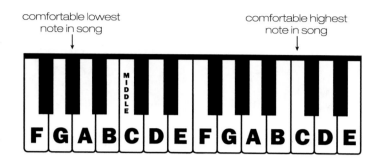

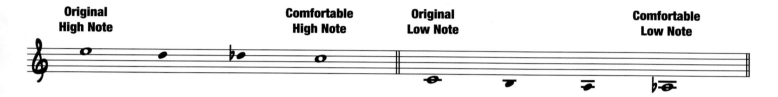

3. Transpose the melody, key signature and chord changes.

Let's say you've determined that the song will be in a better range for you if it is lowered by four half steps (down a minor third). First, transpose the key signature to one that is four steps lower, and write the chord changes in the new key by simply transposing each of them down by four half steps. Then, write in the transposed melody also. (You will probably find it helpful to use the keyboard on pages 4 and 5 when transposing.)

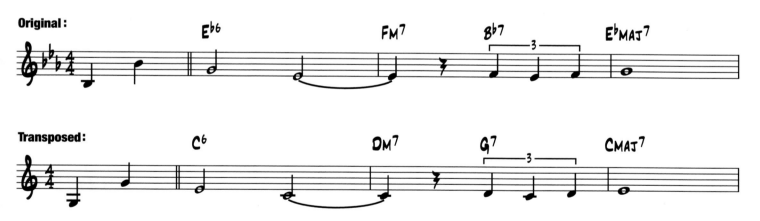

Write It!
Using "Look for the Silver Lining" (or another song of your choosing), transpose it to another key by writing the transposed chords above each of the original chords. Then, write a single stave, chords and slashes lead sheet for the song in the new key.

Check Your Lead Sheet

After writing a lead sheet, it's important to check it for mistakes. The time you take to check your work *now* may save you from having a train wreck on a gig *later*! Count measures: if you find the last A section is only seven bars long, then you probably omitted a measure somewhere. Peruse the chord symbols: if you see several instances of Fm7 - Bb7, but only one instance of Fm7 - B7, then you probably forgot to add the flat to the Bb7 chord. It's ideal if you can check the lead sheet by playing it at the piano. If your jazz piano skills aren't up to the task, then play just the bass notes of the chords on the piano while singing the song; this will sometimes uncover transposition or other mistakes. Or in lieu of that, have a friend play it.

If the tune used as the basis for your lead sheet was taken from an older published fake book, then unfortunately the chord changes could be "buggy." (Incorrect, incomplete, ambiguous, and so on.) In some fake books, the chord symbols were devised from literal interpretations of written out piano renditions, without consideration for how they should be adapted for use in a jazz setting. Therefore, you may find wrong chords, extraneous chord symbols, unclear placement of chord symbols in terms of the beat where they are to occur, and no regard to page layout or double bars helping to delineate the dividing lines between sections. It's *not* a good idea to model these lead sheets exactly as they are written!

There will be a limit to how much editing you can do to fix a "buggy" lead sheet until you learn basic jazz piano. However, you certainly can adjust the page layout, add repeat signs and double bars as necessary, and peruse the chord symbols trying to spot anything that looks suspect. Also, you can clarify the exact placement of chord symbols, keeping in mind that in most cases where there are two chords per measure, the chord symbols will fall on beats one or three. (Again, think even numbers!)

If you don't feel qualified to correct faulty chord progressions yourself, ask a jazz piano or guitar player friend for assistance. One obvious recurring issue that can be easily corrected is chord symbol redundancy: if you see a measure containing C, C6 then back to C, it's probably best to use only one of those three. Luckily, many of the more contemporary fake books, such as those published by Sher Music, contain clear, correct, jazz-appropriate chord symbols.

chapter 10 CREATING AN ARRANGEMENT

A lead sheet can be expanded into an *arrangement* with the addition of a written introduction and ending, and possibly any number of other creative elements such as rhythmic kicks.

TIP An arranged lead sheet is commonly referred to as a *chart*.

Intros

One of the primary purposes of an intro is to set up the style and mood of the song; the intro's character should match the flavor of the tune. Intros for ballads are typically four bars long, while medium- to fast-tempo tunes normally have intros that are at least eight, and occasionally 16 bars long. Below is a catalog of various intros which can be used by transposing them to the key of your lead sheet. *Any of the four-bar intros can be expanded to eight bars by simply using a repeat sign.*

1. Turnaround Intros

Turnarounds are short chord progressions that cycle through the circle of fifths . They can be repeated indefinitely to serve for example as a backdrop for making announcements.

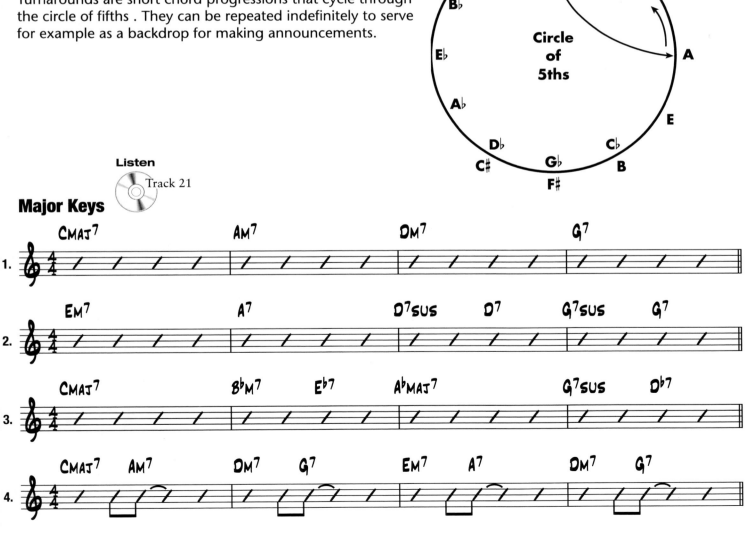

Listen Track 21

Major Keys

2. Vamp Intros

Vamp intros are comprised of two or three chords which repeat three to four times or more. Vamps usually have a predetermined number of repetitions when used as an intro, though they can easily be extended to repeat indefinitely.

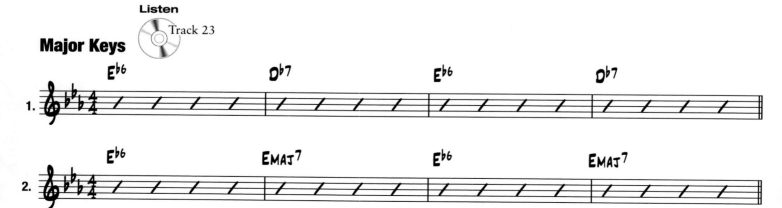

Minor Keys

TIP On rubato ballads, a simple V7 chord with a fermata can be used as a lead into the song in lieu of an intro.

3. Pedal-Tone Intros

Pedal-tone intros have a single bass note, usually the root or the fifth of the key center, underneath changing chords above. Pedal tones tend to generate excitement because of the tension of changing chords over a stationary bass note.

TIP Any rhythmic kicks you see in these intros are optional: using simple quarter-note slashes would also work well. For more information about writing rhythmic kicks, see page 62.

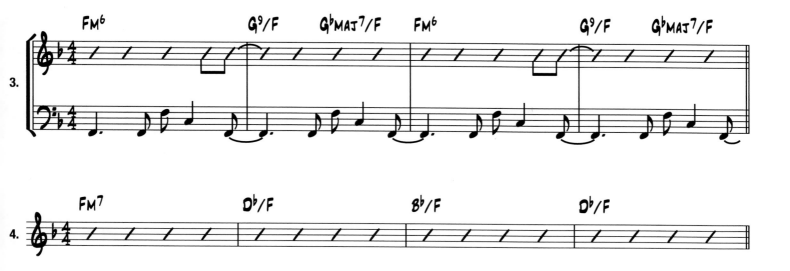

4. Intros for Blues

The most common intro for 12-bar blues tunes is the playing of a chorus (or more) of the blues progression before the tune starts. (See Chapter 8 for more about blues song form and chord progression.)

5. Miscellaneous Intros

There are virtually limitless possibilities for using chord progressions in a creative way to devise intros. Many of the examples here combine elements of the previous intros.

Listen
Track 27

Major Keys

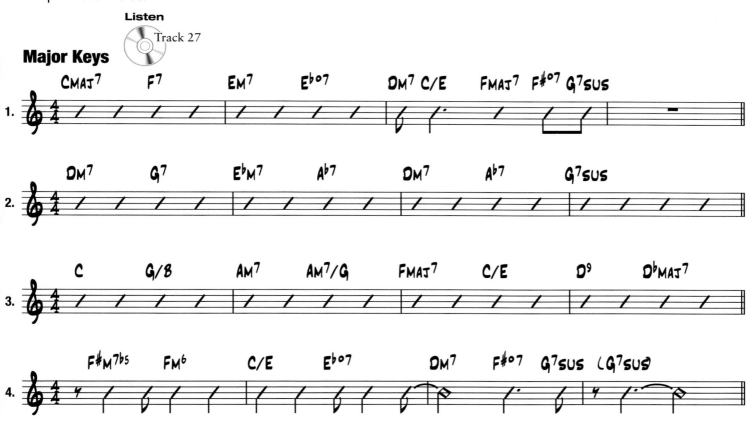

Using a song of your choosing (taken from a jazz fakebook), decide what key would be best suited to your vocal range and write out a transposed, chords and slashes lead sheet for it, with intro.

Listen
Track 28

Minor Keys

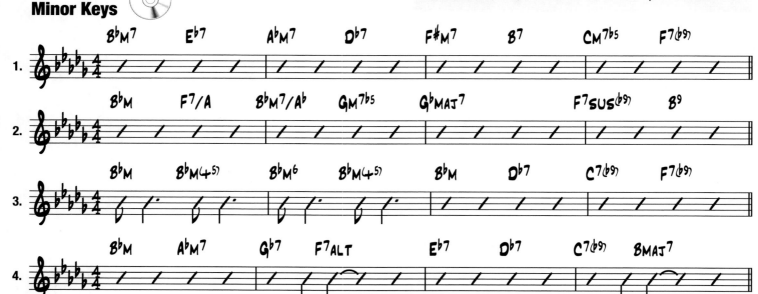

6. Intros for Special Harmonic Situations

A. Intros for Songs That Start on the II Chord

Numerous songs start on the II chord of the song's key. For example, "Honeysuckle Rose," (IIm7), "Our Love is Here to Stay," (II7), and "I Love You," (IIm7b5.) In most of these cases, it will work well to write any turnaround, vamp, or pedal-tone intro. Or, you can write an intro that more specifically leads the ear to the II chord such as in these examples:

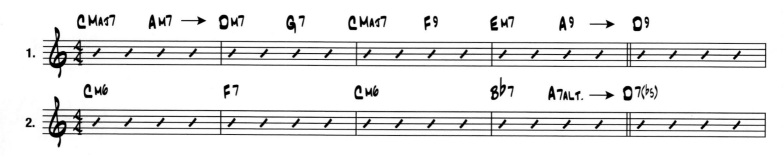

B. Intros for Songs that Start and End in Different Key Centers

Some songs begin in a temporary implied key center that is different than the actual key center of the song, usually represented by the song's final chord. This raises the question of what key to use for the intro. For example, "My Funny Valentine" begins in C minor, but ends in E-flat major. In this particular case, the C minor tonality is well established because it lasts for almost 16 measures. For that reason you would want to write the intro in C minor.

In another example, the song "After You've Gone" begins with the implied key center of B-flat major, but ends in F major. (See "After You've Gone" in Chapter One.) In this case, the B-flat tonality is not well established because it lasts for only a measure or two. For this song you would write the intro in F, but use a transition chord (the V7 or IIm7 - V7 of the chord you're going to) at the very end to guide the ear to the B-flat starting chord.

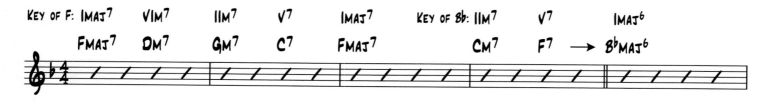

The bottom line is this: the written intro needs to lead your ear to the first chord of the song. Before writing an intro, take a moment to examine what's going on harmonically in the beginning and end of the song, then devise the intro accordingly. Well-known tunes that have different starting and ending keys include "Autumn Leaves," "Fly Me to the Moon," "Just Friends," "Lover Man," "All the Things You Are," "Cry Me a River," "Lullaby of Birdland," "Sweet Georgia Brown" and many others.

Tip *In most cases it works well to use the last four or eight measures of a song as the song's intro.*

Write It!
Using "Fly Me to the Moon," "Lullaby of Birdland," or "Cry Me a River" (any of which can be easily found in a jazz fakebook), decide what key would be best suited to your vocal range and write out a transposed, chords and slashes lead sheet for it, with intro. (Take care with the intro: each of these songs begin and end in different keys.)

Endings

Unlike simple intros such as turnarounds and vamps, written endings can be a little tricky to devise. The chords used for any ending must be written with consideration to the original chord structure of each song. Though there is no set formula that works in every case, we can categorize the most common types of endings, and apply them to a few specific tune examples.

1. Tag Endings

The most common type of ending for jazz standards is a tag ending. A two-time tag is the repetition of the last phrase of the song, twice:

Listen
Track 29

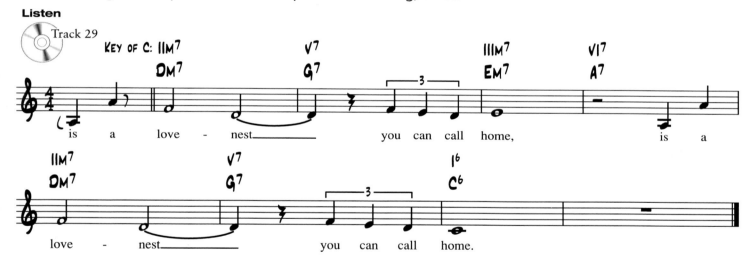

Notice how the melody has been adjusted the first time the word "home" is sung to give it a sense of *continuation* rather than *conclusion*.

A three-time tag is the repetition of only *part* of the last phrase, three times:

There can be a fair amount of variation in the chord changes used for two- and three-time tag endings. Here's another example of a two-time tag:

Here's a variation on the three-time tag:

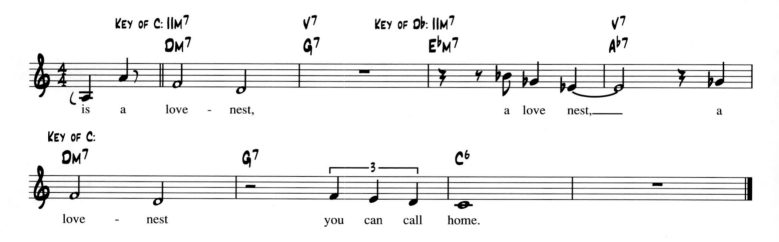

Notice in the above example how the melody has been adjusted to accommodate the new chord changes.

The best way to write a tag ending is to first decide how you would want to *sing* it based on the models above, *then* find the appropriate chords. Numerous songs end with the chord progression IIm7 - V7 - I, *or some variation of it*. In these cases, use the example endings above as models when writing your tag: simply transpose the chords to the key of your song.

Tip If the original ending phrase of the song is four bars long, then the addition of the tag will make the ending twice as long: a total of eight bars. If the original ending was two bars long, then the tag will be a total of four, and so on.

2. Vamp Endings

A vamp ending is the repetition of the last phrase of a song, three to four times or more. The chords of a vamp ending are just like those of a vamp intro: two or more chords which repeat. The vamp can have a predetermined length, or it can be open ended, in which case you'll have to cue the final ending point. Here are examples of both styles:

Listen

Track 30

Notice that in the above examples, a final chord with a fermata is written to represent the conclusion of the vamp and the final ending point of the tune. Any of the chords used for vamp intros can also be used as vamp endings. (See "Vamp Intros" on page 52.)

3. Endings for Ballads

Though tag endings can be used on ballads, they are not your only choice. A ballad with no tag, but a simple *ritard* and one or more held chords at the end is common and works well. Here are two examples:

Listen

Track 31

The two little lines at a slant are called *railroad tracks*. They indicate for the rhythm section to pause, momentarily. Notice the diamond shapes that represent half and whole notes. When using a single stave lead sheet with chords and slashes only, it's a good idea to write the text underneath the stave to help the players follow the vocalist during a ritard or fermata:

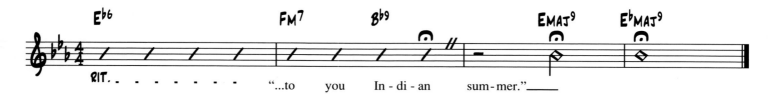

Write It!

Using the last four bars of "Look For the Silver Lining," write out two different endings for it: a two-time tag, and a three-time tag. Remember that each of the tag endings should be a total of eight bars in length. (Twice as long as the original phrase.)

TIP

Some ballads lend themselves to a longer, different type of tag: the one-time repetition of the last eight bars or more of the song. For example, on the song, "People," it works well to sing the entire song, jump back to the text "with one person, one very special person...," then sing the song out to the end again.

Road Map and Other Markings

As your arrangement becomes longer and more detailed, you'll need special markings to help the players navigate through the *road map* and play the chart in the way you would like to hear it, stylistically. Here are some of the most common markings:

1. D.S. (*Dal Segno* in Italian)

This extremely common marking is normally placed at the end of the first chorus of a song, indicating to repeat back to *the sign*. The sign 𝄋 is most often placed at the beginning of the song after the intro, but is sometimes placed at the song's exact middle point. (See "One Note Samba," page 69.)

2. D.C. (*Da Capo* in Italian)

This marking is also usually placed at the end of the first chorus of the song. It indicates to go back to the *very beginning* of the chart. So, if there is an intro at the beginning of your chart, it will be played again if you've written a D.C. Using D.C. is less common than using D.S.

3. Coda

The coda section is an added section of music, usually occurring at the end of the tune. This is where your tag or other ending will be. There are always two *coda signs* ⊕ associated with a coda section. The first coda sign usually appears somewhere in the last eight bars of the tune, indicating to skip directly to the coda *section*. The 2nd coda sign is found at the beginning of the coda section, simply identifying it *as* the coda section. Coda signs are to be observed only after the D.S., D.C., or repeat signs have already been observed. (See "Fly Me to the Moon," page 67.)

TIP

Make sure all markings are large and dark enough to be easily noticed. There could be poor lighting in the club, and you *really* don't want the pianist to miss the coda!

Road map markings can be a little confusing at first. Here's a quick reference to the meanings of each marking, as well as combinations and variations:

    a. D.S: go back to the D.S. sign.

    b. D.C: go back to the very beginning of the tune.

    c. D.S. al Coda: go back to the D.S. sign, play through until you see the coda sign, then skip to the coda section.

    d. D.C. al Coda: go back to the very beginning of the tune, play through until you see the coda sign, then skip to the coda section.

    e. D.S. for solos, last X to Coda: go back to the D.S. sign, and sing or have the instrumentalists play an open number of improvised solo choruses of the song. On the final time through the song (when the melody is sung again), play through until you see the coda sign and then skip to the coda section.

Sometimes you will encounter more elaborate uses of these markings, such as multiple D.S. or Coda signs. This lends itself to potentially confusing instruction, such as "D.S. al 2nd ending al Coda Two." Occasionally it may be necessary in elaborate arrangements to use fairly complex instruction, but in most cases, this is best avoided! Writing out additional sections long hand can alleviate the need for players to have a Ph.D. in chart interpretation. In other words, it's better to have a four-pager that's readable than a three-pager that no one can follow.

TIP Avoid redundancy! Don't use *both* repeat signs and a D.S. to indicate the same thing.

4. Rehearsal Letters

Rehearsal letters are used to provide easy reference to certain spots in the music during a rehearsal. You probably will not need them on most lead sheets and very simple arrangements. Rehearsal letters can be confusing on short lead sheets because, for example, its unclear whether a written letter "B" would be referring to the *B section of the tune*, or *rehearsal letter B*. Be aware that some published fake books do use rehearsal letters as normal practice, even on short lead sheets. Those rehearsal letters however don't need to be copied onto *your* lead sheet unless you feel they would be useful.

For more involved arrangements (when rehearsal letters are necessary), they should be placed above the top stave directly over a bar line at the beginning of a new section. Rehearsal letters are usually enclosed in a box to help make them easily identifiable: | B |

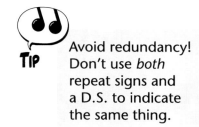

TIP To make your repeat signs as clear as possible when writing charts by hand, add brackets to make them more noticeable.

5. Written Instructions

It's often necessary to write verbal instructions to the players, such as "play 3 times," "2" feel, "4" feel, "rubato," "a tempo," "double-time feel," "a la Freddie Green," or specifically for the drummer, "brushes," "mallets," and so on. Such instructions should be written above the stave, close enough to it so there's no confusion about which stave the instruction applies to. If there's not enough clear space to write the instruction above the staff, it can be written below. Bracketing the text will help make the instruction clearly identifiable: ("2" FEEL)

Write It!

    Using "After You've Gone" (or another song of your choosing), write a chords and slashes lead sheet for it, with intro. Then, use road-map markings to indicate a repeat back to either the intro, beginning of the tune, or second half of the tune (your choice), and then to take the Coda. Create a Coda section containing a vamp ending.

Creative Arrangement Ideas

It would be easy to devote an entire book to ideas for making creative arrangements out of jazz standards, but unfortunately that's out of the scope of this publication! However, here are a few ideas to get you started:

1. Rhythmic Kicks

Adding a few specific *rhythmic kicks* can be a quick and easy way to spice up your chart, giving it a more *arranged* quality. (A *rhythmic kick* is simply a particular rhythm played by the drummer and/or all of the rhythm section players. It can be as brief as a single eighth-note, or as long as two measures or more.) Rhythmic kicks are notated with slashes (representing beats) and stems. Kicks are a fairly common feature of written intros and endings.

Notice that the example above ends with a *rhythmic break*. (A *rhythmic break* is when all players stop playing for a measure or two. The break starts with the playing of a strongly accented chord, most often occurring on beat one or the "and" of four.) Kicks can also be very useful in the main body of a song. Here's an example of the kicks that are commonly played for the first half of "Autumn Leaves":

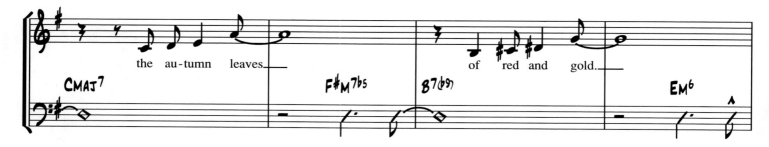

2. Changes in Rhythmic Feel

You could, for example, make the A section of a tune bossa, and the B section swing. Or, do the whole first chorus bossa, going to swing for the solos section. To indicate these changes in rhythmic feel, simply write "Swing" or "Bossa" as appropriate above the measure where you want it.

3. Tempo Changes

A common example of a tempo change is when a ballad starts out rubato, then goes into a slow tempo after the first eight or 16 bars. In this case, you would simply write the word "tempo" or "ballad tempo" above the measure where you'd like it to occur. In other cases, it may be necessary to write a metronome marking (such as ♩ = 152) above the measure where a new tempo begins.

Another common type of tempo change is to go to *double-time* (twice as fast) or *half-time* (half as fast.) For example, if your tune is medium swing, you could add a second chorus of the melody just after the first and write in the words, *double time*. Later in the arrangement, you may want to go back to *half time*. Double time is often accompanied by the following marking:

For half time, the marking is reversed:

TIP

Double-time *feel* differs from double time in that the players make the rhythms *feel* as though the tempo is twice as fast, but the chords and melody actually go by at the same rate of speed. In a double-time feel, each measure *feels* like it's two measures. The opposite is true for half-time *feel*; each measure *feels* like it's only half a measure.

4. Meter Changes

Have you ever tried singing "Autumn Leaves" as a jazz waltz? Nor have I, but the concept of changing the meter of a song can work quite well and breathe new life into the tune! Here's an example of "Autumn Leaves" as a jazz waltz:

Or, it also works well in 5/4:

5. Modulations

Modulating (changing keys) is a great way to create interest in your arrangement. The most common modulations are up a half-step or whole-step, both of which give an energy boost and create a dramatic effect. Another very useful modulation is to change to the key center that is a minor or major third below the original key center. For example, modulating from the key of A-flat to the key of F.

Modulations are usually (but not *necessarily*) prepared by the insertion of a V7 chord (or IIm7 - V7) of *the chord you're going to* in the new key. This harmonic preparation should occur one or two measures before the new key actually starts. Here's an example of the last line of "My Honey's Lovin' Arms," with a modulation into the beginning of the tune in a new key:

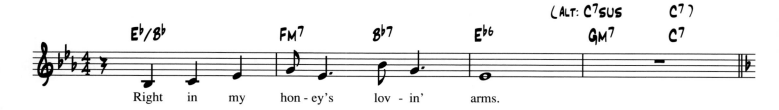

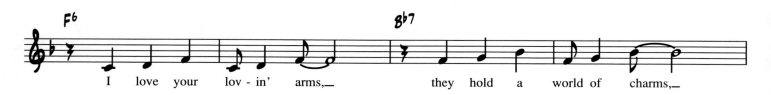

Never bring an arrangement to a rehearsal or gig until you have a good sense of what it will sound like and how to sing it. This is where your piano skills could really come in handy!

Sample Charts

The following charts are provided to show you examples of simple arrangements of jazz standard tunes, with common features such as intros and endings. Each chart is recorded on the CD, allowing you to practice the songs with their corresponding tracks. Though the melody and lyrics are not written here, each of these standard songs can easily be found in published fake books or online through digital download services. (See Appendix III)

ROUTE 66

This track features four choruses of 12-bar blues, with a 4-bar intro, and a 3x tag ending. The rhythmic groove is a *shuffle*, and since Route 66 is a based on a blues progression, you can also use this track to practice other blues tunes. (For further information on the musical characteristics of this track, refer to Chapter 13, "Shuffle.")

SUMMERTIME

 Track 33

This well-known tune is played as a funk ballad. It has an 8-bar vamp intro, and a 2x tag ending which is followed by an additional vamp to finish out the song. (On the final vamp, simply repeat the words, "don't you cry.") The song form is ABAC, with each section being only four bars long. However, since the song is always performed twice to accommodate both verses of lyrics, the song length tends to *feel* like a normal, 32-bar tune. (For further information on the musical characteristics of this track, refer to Chapter 13, "Funk Ballad.")

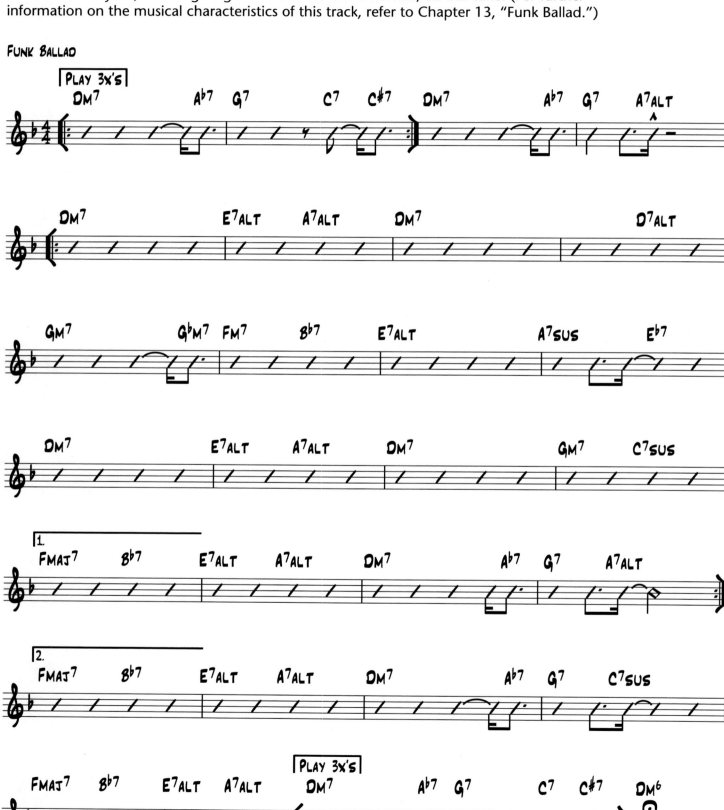

FLY ME TO THE MOON

 Track 34

This track is in a bright swing feel. The first chorus is played with a "2" feel, and the second, in "4." There is an 8-bar pedal tone intro, and a 3x tag ending. The song form is ABAB. (For further information on the musical characteristics of this track, refer to Chapter 13, "Swing, 2 feel.")

God Bless the Child

 Track 35

This song is played in a $\frac{12}{8}$ feel, and has a 4-bar intro. It is a chorus and a half in length: at the end of the first chorus, you will return to the bridge and sing again to the end. *Notice how the chord changes have been adjusted at the end of the first chorus to help transition back to the first chord of the bridge.* There is no tag or other type of ending where phrases are repeated, only a ritard and fermatas. The song form is AABA, but the A sections are each 10 bars long. (For further information on the musical characteristics of this track, refer to Chapter 13, "$\frac{12}{8}$ Ballad.")

RIT. - - -"...THAT'S GOT HIS OWN."

ONE NOTE SAMBA

Track 36

This samba track has a vamp intro and a 3x tag. The song form is AABA,
but the A sections are 16 bars each. (For further information on the
musical characteristics of this track, refer to Chapter 13, "Samba.")

Sample Arrangements

Below are two very different arrangements of the tune, "The Love Nest," provided to give you examples of how a song can be transformed through creative elements of arranging. It is recommended that you listen to the recording on the CD while studying the arranging elements of these tracks; each measure is numbered for easy reference to particular places in the charts. The vocal demonstration is recorded on one stereo side so you can listen to it to learn the arrangements, then turn it off (via the balance knob on your stereo) to sing with the track yourself. (These arrangements are intended for demonstration and practice purposes only; if used for performance they would need to be lengthened by the use of D.S. or other markings.)

Arrangement I: *The Love Nest*

Mood/Feeling: Sensitive, transparent, buoyant, gentle, intimate

Rhythmic Groove: Jazz waltz, played with a feeling of one beat per measure.

Intro: Pedal Tone, mm. 1–8.

Ending: Repetition of final phrase, "you can call home," three times, mm. 57–68. It's essentially a tag ending because of the repetition of the lyrics, but the chords are not characteristic of a "normal" tag.

Chord Changes: The A sections are reharmonized by use of a pedal tone with changing chords above, creating a feeling of suspense. (*Re-harmonizing* means to make creative alterations in the chord changes of a song.) Also, at mm. 29–36, mm. 49–52 and mm. 57–68, the chords are devised with a linear bass line that moves by step. These passages help to provide thematic unity in the arrangement.

Other Arranging Devices:

1. Extended final phrase, .." is a Love Nest..." mm. 49–56. The original phrase was two measures long, but in this arrangement it's now eight bars.

2. The dynamics written in m. 9, 17, 25 and so on help to create a dramatic build in each of the A sections.

3. Rhythmic Kicks: mm. 9–24, mm. 49–56, and letter D. (Notice that rehearsal letters are placed on this chart!)

Track 37

THE LOVE NEST

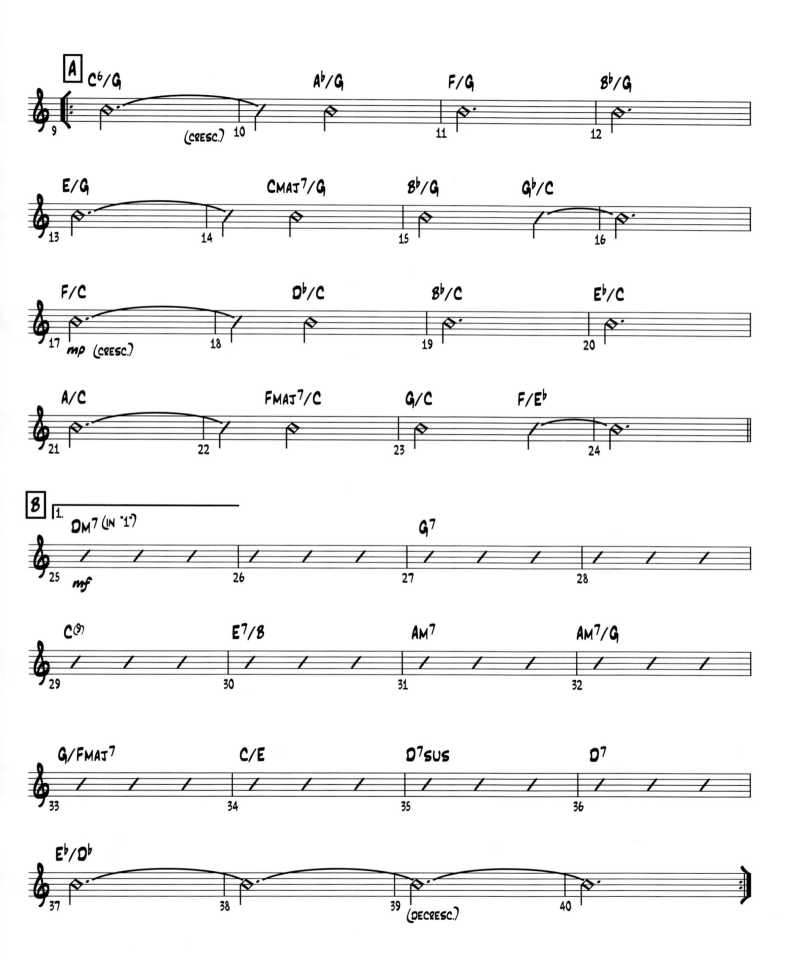

Arrangement II: *The Love Nest*

Mood/Feeling: Bluesy, playful, strong/assertive, earthy, soulful, rhythmic

Rhythmic Groove: Shuffle

Intro: Vamp mm. 1–8. The chord progression C7–Bb7 is widely known as "Killer Joe changes," stemming from its characteristic sound in the song, "Killer Joe." Notice there are rhythmic kicks as part of the intro.

Ending: Extended tag, mm. 29–42. This tag is similar to a 3x time tag, but the phrase "is a Love Nest" is repeated a total of seven times. After the tag there is a vamp on the words, "you can call home," mm. 42–46.

Chord Changes: Reharmonized to create a blusey feeling through the use of dominant 7th chords and classic blues-based harmonic cliche's, such as at m. 8 and m. 41.

Other Arranging Devices:

1. Rhythmic kicks throughout the chart.

2. Rhythmic breaks at m. 23, 41, and 46.

The Love Nest

Track 38

chapter **11** ORGANIZING A GIG BOOK

You'll need to have a gig book if you plan to work professionally as a singer. Your basic gig book should contain lead sheets and simple charts, not elaborate arrangements. The idea is to have all the charts in your book well written and easy to sight-read. However, if you're preparing for concerts or recording, you might have need for more elaborate charts, and in this case a separate gig book could be created for that purpose. Or, you could file the more complicated arrangements behind basic versions of the same tunes in your regular gig book, available for use if needed.

There are at least two different styles of gig books, both of which are commonly used. The three-ring binder gig book style described below is the one I believe to be the most practical for general gig situations. It works!

The Table of Contents

The table of contents is for quick reference to the tunes in the gig book. In your table of contents, list the song title and key, specifying minor keys as necessary. List the songs in alphabetical order, grouped together by style. In other words, list all of your swing tunes in alphabetical order under the *swing* category, and all of your ballads and bossas the same way. You may also have need for additional categories such as *Rock*, *Broadway*, or *Other* which might include odd meter or original tunes. It's not uncommon to have 150–250 songs in a jazz gig book, though you can certainly start with a much smaller number and simply add more over time. (See page 75).

Three-Ring Binder Gig Book

Buy a large three-ring binder and a couple of packages of plastic sleeves to insert in the binder. Put all of your tunes in the sleeves and arrange them in alphabetical order, with the table of contents in the front. As you add new charts, simply insert them in alphabetical order, and update the table of contents. Ultimately, you'll need to create at least three copies of your gig book if you plan to work with a rhythm section.

It's important to show two-page charts appearing on the left and right sides of the open binder, respectively. For charts that are three or more pages, place the whole thing inside one of the plastic sleeves

with the front page of the chart showing. You'll have to remember to instruct the players to take it out of the sleeve when you call the tune. (Some singers prefer to have all pages of a "three-pager" show in the plastic sleeves, requiring a page turn for the players. Either way can work; it's a matter of preference.) If you have alternate versions of the same tune, such as one for regular gigs and a more elaborate one for concerts, write the abbreviation "alt." on the alternate chart so that it is never confused with the basic chart. Don't forget to list the alternate version in the table of contents.

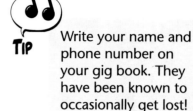

Tip Write your name and phone number on your gig book. They have been known to occasionally get lost!

Loose-Leaf Folder Gig Book

Another common gig book style is the loose-leaf folder book. In this type of book, each chart is numbered and pulled out for use when needed. The table of contents is in alphabetical order, listing the song name, key, chart number and style. You may wish to have a secondary table of contents which also separates the tunes into style categories.

The loose-leaf folder gig book has the advantage of allowing you to have over several hundred charts, all in one place. But the disadvantage is that over time, charts can get lost or tattered because of the constant hands-on use. Also, all of the charts that are pulled out for use on a gig will later need to be refiled, by *someone*!

Many music stores carry large folders designed for this type of gig book, and again, you'll need a copy for each of the rhythm section players. Your name and/or the name of an instrument (piano, bass or drums for example) can be embossed onto the folder.

Tip Many singers create a separate *lyrics only* book for themselves. It can be difficult to stay fresh on the words to 200 tunes!

Song List

Swing Tunes

Key	Song
Db	A Foggy Day
G	All of Me
Eb	All of You
Ab	April In Paris
Ab	At Long Last Love
Dm	Autumn Leaves
Bb	Beautiful Friendship
C	Bye Bye Blackbird
Ab	Cheek to Cheek
Eb	Darn That Dream
Ab	Dearly Beloved
Ab	Dearly Beloved (alt.)
Ab	Fly Me to the Moon
Bb	Give Me the Simple Life
C	Honeysuckle Rose
F	How High the Moon
F	I Remember You
C	I Thought About You
Db	If I Were a Bell
C	I'm Beginning to See the Light
Eb	I'm Old Fashoined
Eb	I'm Old Fashoined (alt.)
Eb	It Could Happen to You
Eb	Just Friends
Bb	Just In Time
G	Like Someone In Love
Eb	Long Ago and Far Away
Db	Love Is Here to Stay
F	Lullaby of Birdland
Bb	Masquerade Is Over, The
Bb	My Romance
Eb	Red Top
Eb	Route 66
Db	Secret Love
Ab	Song Is You, The
Eb	Speak Low
Bb	Star Eyes
Bbm	Sugar
Dm	Summertime
Bb	Teach Me Tonight
Db	They Can't Take That Away
Eb	This Can't Be Love
Bb	Time After Time
Eb	When Your Lover Is Gone
Am	Yesterdays

Ballads

Key	Song
Bbm	Angel Eyes
Eb	Black Coffee
Bb	Body and Soul
Bb	Body and Soul (alt.)
Eb	But Beautiful
Am	Cry Me a River
Bb	Everytime We Say Goodbye
Bb	Georgia
Eb	It Might As Well Be Spring
Ab	My Foolish Heart
Bbm	My Funny Valentine
Em/G	Shadow of Your Smile, The
Eb	Since I Fell for You
Bb	Skylark
Eb	Tea for Two
Bbm	Thrill Is Gone, The
Fm	What Are You Doing the Rest of Your Life
Eb	When I Fall In Love
F	When Sunny Gets Blue
Eb	Willow Weep for Me
Cm	You Don't Know What Love Is
C	You've Changed

Latin Tunes

Key	Song
Bb	Corcorvado
F	Desifinado
C	Dindi
Dm	Estate
Ab	Fascinatin' Rhythm
Ab	Fascinatin' Rhythm (alt.)
Am	Gentle Rain
Bbm	How Insensitive
C	Night and Day
Dm	No More Blues
Bb	One Note Samba
Bb	Someone to Light Up My Life
Db	Songbird
Eb	Speak Low
F	Summer Samba (So Nice)
C	Watch What Happens
F	Wave

TIP You may actually know many more songs than are represented in your gig book. Making a complete list of *all* the jazz tunes you can sing will remind you of tunes you could call on a gig that aren't in your book, as long as the players know them.

chapter 12 REHEARSING A RHYTHM SECTION

Special performances such as concerts or recordings may require a rehearsal with the rhythm section. The purpose of a rehearsal is not to simply run through the tunes, but rather to work through any spots in the arrangements that require special attention. You should consider yourself the leader in this situation, facilitating the rehearsal and guiding the players in making musical sense of the charts.

Preparation, Preparation, Preparation

This is what I refer to with my students as "the three P's." If you are well prepared for the rehearsal, the chances are you'll meet all of your rehearsal goals and make efficient use of the time, something the players will greatly appreciate. Preparation should include making sure charts are well written, copied and taped if need be; arranging the rehearsal space; making sure there are music stands if needed; knowing what grooves and tempos you want; practicing count-offs ahead of time if necessary; knowing the arrangements you wrote and being aware of problem spots in the charts and so on.

Talking Down the Chart

For charts that have tricky passages or a complicated road map, be prepared to talk down the chart: simply look through the chart with the rhythm section before it is played, talking through the road map and pointing out any particulars in the arrangement that require extra attention. You may want to rehearse one or more complicated sections of the chart before playing/ singing through the whole thing.

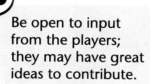

TIP Be open to input from the players; they may have great ideas to contribute.

Counting off Tunes

As the leader, you will be responsible for counting off the songs. Each rhythmic style and tempo will of course call for a different style of count off. Make sure your count off is in the same *character* of the tune you're about to sing. For example, on a joyful, bright swing tune, the count off should have the same energized flavor. Be sure that all players *hear* your count off, not just the pianist. Look around; if the drummer is still pulling out his or her brushes, you're not ready to start the tune yet! Track 39 is provided for you to hear examples of count offs for the most common rhythmic styles in jazz.

Listen

 Track 39

TIP Don't be in a hurry to count off your tune; this can be a fatal error! First, hear the melody and words in your head to make absolutely sure you have the tempo you want. *Then,* count it off.

About the Instruments

This section provides basic info about the roles and capabilities of the rhythm section instruments. It would be impossible to catalog a complete list of *all* idiomatic characteristics of each instrument, but many of the most common are described here. Much of the info below is demonstrated on the CD in various tracks. (See Chapter 13, "Rhythmic Grooves and Playing Styles.")

1. Piano and Guitar

The primary roles of the pianist and guitar player are to *comp* and to solo. (The word *comp* is derived from *accompanying* or *complementing*, and it refers to the playing of rootless chord voicings. Players *comp* when there is a bass player present who is playing the roots of the chords.) The pianist or guitar player makes a key contribution to the sound of the musical whole through their individual style of comping, specifically in their *voicings* (the arrangement of the notes in a chord) and their rhythmic choices. These players may also interject melodic or chordal fills, and can be called upon to play specific written parts.

It's not uncommon to make special musical requests of the rhythm section players. For example, you might ask the pianist or guitar player to play a busier or more sparse comping style, more or fewer melodic fills, or perhaps fills that have a certain flavor, such as bluesy fills. For bossa novas, you might ask the guitarist to play acoustic (nylon string) guitar if he or she has it. Other particulars include asking the pianist to play a *Basie ending*, or the guitarist to play in a *Freddie Green* style. (See Chapter 13, "Rhythmic Grooves and Playing Styles.")

2. Bass

The bass player is the link between harmony and rhythm; he or she is at the foundation of both. On swing tunes, you may ask the bass player for a *"2" feel* at the beginning, and to *walk* at the bridge or perhaps on the second chorus. (A *"2" feel* is characterized by the playing of roots of the chords on beats one and three only, giving the music a feeling of two beats per measure. A *walking bass line* is characterized by the predominant use of four quarter notes in each measure. Walking bass lines are *in "4."*) For Latin tunes or rock ballads, the use of an electric bass is optional.

3. Drums

The drummer is responsible not only for laying down a good sense of time and rhythmic feel, but also for being the energy hub of the rhythm section. The drummer has potential to play a great variety of textures, patterns and sound *colors*. All musicians (singers included!) should know the names of each part of the drumset.

You can specify whether you want the drummer to play with sticks or brushes for a particular tune, though if nothing is said, he or she will probably play sticks for swing and Latin tunes, and brushes for ballads. Or, you may want a combination of the two, asking the drummer (for example) to start on brushes and then go to sticks for the solo section.

At the end of a ballad, the drummer will normally play cymbal rolls using either brushes or *mallets* on any held chords. (The *mallets* used by jazz drummers are sticks with felt- or yarn-covered balls at the end which make a warm, "schhhhwaaaaaaaa" sound when used for a cymbal roll.)   Also, it can be a great special effect to have the drummer play mallets on slow Latin tunes, or, to play with their hands on the toms.

Anatomy of a Drumset

The *ride pattern* is the specific rhythm drummers play on the ride cymbal when in swing feel:

Sometimes the ride pattern is played on the hi-hat, a la Buddy Rich. At the beginning of a swing tune, you may want to ask the drummer (along with the bass player) to play a *"2" feel*. This will result in an abbreviated ride pattern which implies a feeling of two beats per measure:

Other possibilities pertaining to the drums include the playing of a *back beat* (the playing of beats two and four strongly on the snare drum when in swing feel to generate a stronger feeling of rhythmic drive), a *cross stick* (hitting the rim of the snare with the middle [approx. 1 ½ to 2 inches from the butt end] of the drum stick as a regular part of a drum pattern), or a *rim shot* (a short and loud crack sounded by hitting the drum so that the stick strikes the drumhead and rim simultaneously.)

Tip If you want the drummer to play a certain, unusual type of groove, the best way to communicate it to them is to sing it using drum-like sounds!

chapter **13** RHYTHMIC GROOVES AND PLAYING STYLES

The following is a catalog and description of the most commonly played jazz grooves (rhythmic styles) and their variations. Most of the grooves are represented on the CD, and it's recommended that while reading each description, you listen to the corresponding CD track. Familiarity with the names and characteristics of each style is important for any jazz musician.

Swing Styles

Listen Track 1

1. Swing Feel

The swing feel here is in "4," with the drummer playing sticks. Notice that the bass player is playing a walking bass line.

Listen Track 34

2. Swing "2" Feel

In this tune, the rhythm section plays a "2" feel for the first chorus, and goes to a "4" feel in the second. The drummer is using sticks. Notice that the bass player is primarily playing on beats one and three during the "2" feel section. On the last several measures of the track, you'll hear a rhythmic break followed by a Basie ending in the piano. (A *Basie ending* is a characteristic ending made famous by the well-known band leader and pianist, Count Basie.)

Listen Track 9

3. Swing (with Freddie Green Style Guitar)

Freddie Green was the long time guitarist in the Count Basie band, and was noted for his style of playing down-stroke quarter notes on all four beats. The drummer is using brushes here.

4. Broken Time Swing Feel

In more contemporary jazz music, the bass player and drummer don't always strictly adhere to their traditional swing playing patterns. The drummer freely interjects fills in this style, and only loosely implies a ride pattern, resulting in a very open and spacial feeling. (No corresponding CD track.)

Latin Styles

Latin is a catchall term for the musical styles from a wide variety of countries. The geographical regions that have been most influential to Latin jazz music are Brazil and the Caribbean.

Listen Track 5

1. Bossa Nova

Bossa nova is a straight-eighth groove from Brazil, popularized by the wealth of great music written by composer, Antonio Carlos Jobim. (*Straight eighths*, also called *even eighths*, are simply eighth notes played as usual, without the underlying triplet feeling of swing.) On this track, the drummer is playing with sticks. Notice the comping rhythm of the guitar: this Brazilian rhythmic pattern is called *partito alto*.

Listen Track 36

2. Samba

Samba is also from Brazil. It has a feeling of two beats per measure and is usually played a little faster than bossa. In this example, the drummer is using brushes.

TIP There are numerous other Latin grooves that are popular with jazz musicians, such as Songo, Mambo and $\frac{6}{8}$ Afro-Latin. Though these styles are not as commonly used by vocalists, you should be aware of them and consider using them for creative arrangements and/or to breathe new life into jazz standard tunes. See Appendix III, Professional Resource Guide for suggested publications to learn more about Latin styles.

Ballad Styles

Listen

 Track 3

1. Jazz Ballad

The drummer uses brushes on this track. Also, notice that the bass player is playing primarily half notes.

> **TIP**   Take care when counting off ballads! On some tunes it's easy to mistakenly count off in half notes as though they were quarter notes. Be sure you are aware of how the feeling of the quarter-note pulse in the accompaniment relates to the melody of the song.

Listen

 Track 35

2. $\frac{12}{8}$ Ballad

The name of this style comes from the fact that each of the four quarter-note beats in the measure are *felt* as triplets, adding up to a total feeling of 12 beats in each measure:

$\frac{12}{8}$ ballads often have a heavier feel and more bluesy flavor than jazz ballads. Notice that the drummer uses sticks here, but goes to mallets to play cymbal rolls for the held chords at the end.

Listen

 Track 7

3. $\frac{12}{8}$ Ballad (with stride piano)

Stride is a solo piano style which was popular in the early decades of the 20th century. In this example, the modified stride piano style is integrated into the rhythm section playing a light $\frac{12}{8}$ feel. The drummer uses brushes.

Listen

 Track 33

4. Funk Ballad

This rhythmic feel is borrowed from the genre of rock music, though the chord progressions and style of playing are still characteristic of jazz. Usually in rock or funk ballads, the bass plays a certain rhythmic pattern that works in conjunction with the drum pattern; there are a multitude of different rhythmic patterns possible. This example represents an underlying sixteenth note subdivision, whereas a rock ballad would have a feeling of eighth-note subdivision. The drummer uses sticks.

Other Styles

Listen

 Track 37

1. Jazz Waltz

Jazz waltz is a ¾ groove, but uses swing eighth notes just as in ¼ swing. In this example, the rhythm section plays with a feeling of "1" (one beat per measure), giving the music a light and buoyant sound. Notice that the bass player predominately plays dotted half notes, while the drummer uses brushes.

Jazz waltz can also be played with a feeling of "3" (three beats per measure), giving a much more driving sense to the music. The bass player *walks* when it's in "3." Or, it's common for a jazz waltz to be in "1" during parts of the song, and in "3" for other parts, very similar to the way "2" and "4" feel are used in swing feel.

Listen

 Track 32

2. Shuffle

Shuffle and swing are very similar, but the shuffle has a heavier, more driving feeling, and leans more toward a subdivision of dotted eighth/sixteenth notes than triplets. Shuffles are also common in blues and rock genres. You'll hear a brief stop-time passage on the third chorus of this track. (*Stop time* is the playing of a series of rhythmic breaks in a passage of music.) The classic ending used here is sometimes referred to as an *Ellington ending*, stemming from its use on the Duke Ellington song, "Take the A Train."

3. Jazz-Rock Groove

This is another straight-eighth groove, familiar to many jazz musicians through the Herbie Hancock tune, "Watermelon Man," originally recorded in the 1970s. This groove has elements of both Latin and rock, and was an early representation of the style that evolved into what was later termed, "Fusion." (No corresponding CD Track.)

TIP There are numerous other non-categorical grooves possible that combine jazz- and rock-based styles. In these cases, it's important to communicate to the bass player and drummer the basic rhythmic pattern and subdivision (eighth note or 16th note) of the groove. You can convey this by writing a couple of measures of the bass part on the beginning of your chart as an example of what you have in mind; this is enough to give both the bass player and drummer the idea. Or, you can sing it to them using drum-like sounds.

chapter **14** SITTING IN

Sitting in refers to performances where you have been invited to sing a song or two on someone else's gig, or where you are participating in an organized jam session. In these unrehearsed situations, it's particularly important that you're able to communicate certain pertinent musical information to the rhythm section ahead of time. You should also be familiar with *the ropes*: the usual order of events during the performance of the song.

Choose Your Song Wisely

Choose a tune that has a high probability of working well in this situation, something that is probably familiar to the players but has not been overdone. Generally you wouldn't use a chart when sitting in, but it never hurts to discreetly bring along a few lead sheets of your tune just in case they may be needed. Also, it's a good idea to have two or three song choices in various styles up your sleeve so you can go to plan B if necessary in case, for example, the person performing just before you sang your song!

Another factor that may go into the song choice includes what you hear to be the strengths of the players. For example, if the pianist has a great touch and a talent for beautiful voicings, you may want to sing a ballad. The overall goal is to choose a song that everyone has the potential to sound great on.

TIP Choosing a tune you are comfortable singing in the original key is a plus: the players will likely be more familiar with it in the original key, increasing the chances they will play it well for you.

What to Tell the Players

When you approach the bandstand, be prepared to give the players the following information: name of the tune, key, rhythmic feel, and tempo. Then briefly talk with the piano player about what type of intro you want. With experienced pros, you can simply ask for four bars up front if it's a ballad, or eight bars up front if the song is in a medium or fast tempo. If you prefer to know exactly what you're going to get for an intro, you can specify the chord changes to

be played. For example, you could ask for a I-VI-II-V-I intro, or a vamp on the chords C7-Bb7. (See "Intros," Chapter 10) It's also common to ask the rhythm section to play the last four or eight bars of the tune as an intro. Specifying the exact intro you want may help you earn more respect from the players for knowing your P's and Q's. But the disadvantage is that it ties their creative hands; left to their own devices, the rhythm section would probably come up with an intro that's more interesting than a basic I-VI-II-V-I turnaround!

In regard to endings, it's common practice to sing a tag or vamp ending on most songs, and this is what the players will probably expect unless they are told otherwise. You can, however, ask for a specific type of ending if you want to be absolutely sure about what they'll play. (See "Endings," Chapter 10)

TIP Talk to the players in their language, using terms like "head," "chorus," "A section," "bridge" and "tag." (If in doubt about the meaning of a word, look it up in the index to find its definition.)

The Ropes

Here's a rundown of the typical order of events when sitting in:

1. You call the tune, key, tempo and rhythmic feel. To indicate your tempo, snap or lightly clap quarter notes in rhythm, snapping all four beats for bossa and beats two and four only for swing tunes. (Omit the snaps entirely for ballads.)

    Example jargon: "Hi. Let's do 'All of Me' in F, medium swing, about here." (Snap or tap the tempo you have in mind.) "Please play the last eight for an intro."

2. Count off the tune, or invite the pianist to count it off. But, don't be surprised if once you've given the tempo, the players launch right into the intro before you have a chance to count it off for them; each situation is different depending on the players involved. The advantage of you counting off the tune is that it gives players the message

that you know what you're doing, which helps to build musical trust. But, you will have to feel out each situation and be willing to go with the flow. (Listen to **CD Track 39** for examples of count-offs.)

Listen

Track 39

3. Sing the entire melody, after which one or more players will solo, and/or you might *scat sing*. (*Scat singing* is vocal improvisation using syllables.) When a player (or singer) *solos*, they are improvising new melodic lines on the chord progression of the song; *the song form stays intact and simply repeats* as many times as necessary to accommodate the solos.   Be sure to keep track of where you are in the song form during solos; you don't want to get lost and then not know where to come back in with the melody!

Use eye contact to determine who will solo and who will not. It's typical for the pianist or guitarist and one or more horn players to solo for a chorus or more, and less common (but still possible) to have the bass player solo. For medium-tempo songs, there would typically be no more than two or three soloists, and for ballads, one or two. During the instrumental solos, step back and to the side slightly, out of the center stage area.

4. As the final soloist is finishing up (the final soloist being determined by you in this situation), give a nonverbal indication that you'll be coming back in with the melody by slowly stepping back toward the center stage area. Make eye contact as necessary to be sure the players pick up on what's happening.

5. Sing the melody to the end. In most cases you will then sing a tag or vamp ending. You can lead the ending with your voice by assertively *singing any note other than the final tonic note at the end of the song,* indicating you're not done yet and you want to extend the ending. Experienced players should have no problem following you. However if in doubt, move your arm in circles as if to say, "we're going around on this last phrase again." Ballads most often end with a ritard on the final phrase of the song, regardless of whether or not there is a tag. Again, this can be lead vocally and reinforced with body language or conducting gestures if necessary.

TIP On fast tunes, it's common to sing the *head* (the melody) twice.

Visual Cues

Certain situations require more explicate nonverbal cues, such as in open vamp endings when you will need to cue the last time of the cycle to actually end the song. Luckily, with clear visual signals, it's possible to communicate a great deal of musical information! The traditional cue to indicate the final time through an open vamp is to first turn a little sidewise toward the players to get their attention, then raise your arm in the air and make a fist as if to say, "This is the final time; we're taking it out."

Other common visual cues include pointing to the top of your head to indicate you want to return to the melody. Or, if you want a rhythmic break, hold your hand up in the air as if to say, "watch me, something's going to happen," then conduct a strong, accented beat exactly where you want the break. The more clear and assertive you are with your gestures, the more success you will have with visual cues. With experienced players, its not always necessary to use such explicate gestures: some players are so sensitive they will pick up on what you want with a simple glance, and by listening intently to the direction you are going, vocally.

TIP Go with the flow when sitting in. Remember, its an unrehearsed situation, and there may be some surprises. Stay aware, flexible and responsive.

Performance Considerations

This entire publication is geared toward jazz singers becoming better musicians. With this in mind, it's ideal to do what you can to help mitigate the dividing line between singer and accompanists when sitting in. Don't forget that jazz is a team sport! Join the players with a friendly attitude of cooperation and respect.

The question of whether or not to keep your eyes open during performance is widely debated. Some singers feel it's vital to make eye contact with audience members to reach them, emotionally. Others feel it's the emotion in the music that will touch an audience, regardless of what's going on visually. It seems to me that if a singer's eyes are occasionally closed but the listener is still engaged, then there's no fundamental problem. As a matter of fact, sometimes in smaller performance spaces, too much direct eye contact might be uncomfortable for an audience. On the other side of the coin, however, if a singer's eyes are locked shut because of shyness or nerves, it's unlikely that he or she will effectively get their message out to the listener. The bottom line is, whether eyes are open or sometimes closed, the goal is to communicate, and if whatever you're doing isn't working then its time to investigate why.

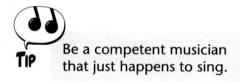
TIP Be a competent musician that just happens to sing.

A Word about Microphone Use

Though it's outside the scope of this publication to go deeply into sound system equipment and usage, a few comments are in order. Hearing your voice through speakers takes some getting used to. Unfortunately, jazz singers are somewhat at the mercy of the quality of the sound system, the natural acoustics of the room, and whomever is running the PA. The biggest potential problem, and one that all jazz singers have experienced at one time or another, is that of not being able to hear yourself well on stage. Unfortunately, this simply *will* happen at some point (or numerous times) in your career, and you will have to manage by operating largely on vocal muscle memory. The problem can be remedied somewhat by stepping in closer toward the stage monitor if there is one, signaling for the sound tech to turn up the monitor volume, and/or signaling to the rhythm section to play a little softer. Also, several sound equipment companies sell little personal monitors that can be very useful on stage, providing there's an opportunity to get it set up and plugged in to the PA prior to the performance.

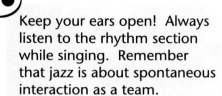
TIP Keep your ears open! Always listen to the rhythm section while singing. Remember that jazz is about spontaneous interaction as a team.

Here are some other guidelines about microphone use:

1. Hold the microphone one to two inches from your lips. If it's too close, the sound may get "woofy," and if it's too far, the vocal tone may be too thin and bright.

2. Pull the mic slightly away from your mouth for particularly loud or high notes.

3. Generally, hold the microphone at about a 45-degree angle. Remember that some microphones are very directional and are greatly affected by the angle at which you sing into it. Always avoid singing into the side of any microphone.

4. Try to get physically comfortable holding the mic, so that it feels natural. Keep your hand relaxed, not gripping the mic too tightly. Shoulders should stay down, and your elbow should stay fairly close to the body.

5. If you find that your "p's" or other plosive consonants are popping, try directing your air stream a little over the top of the mic instead of directly into the center of it.

6. Practice getting comfortable holding a mic by substituting a pen and singing in front of the mirror.

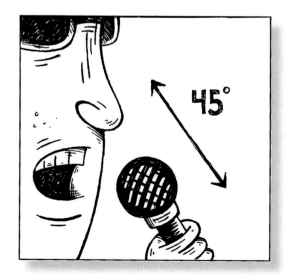

appendix ▌1▐ MUSIC FUNDAMENTALS

Key Signatures

Circle of Fifths

Each of the major keys shown with the relative minor (m).

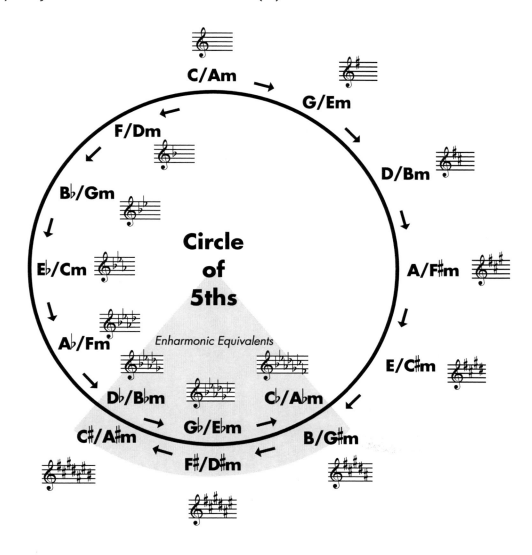

Intervals

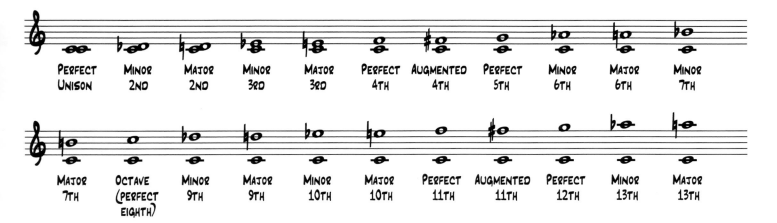

Scales

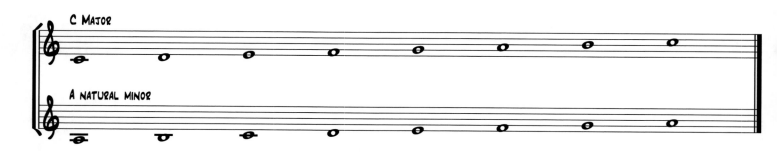

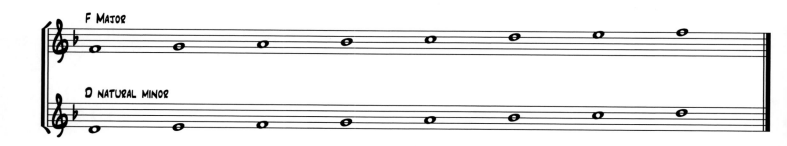

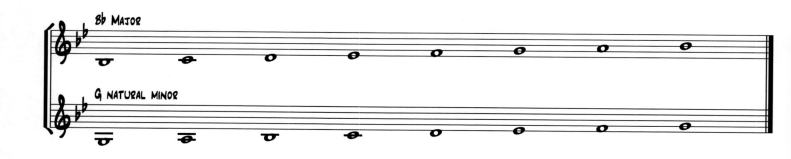

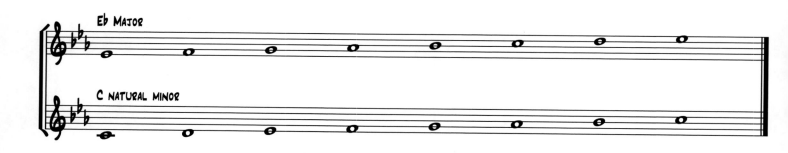

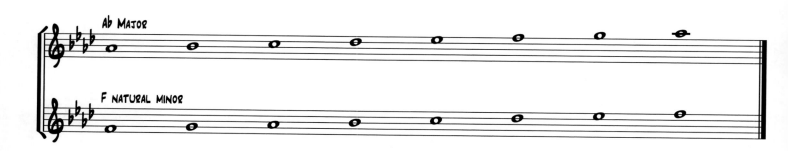

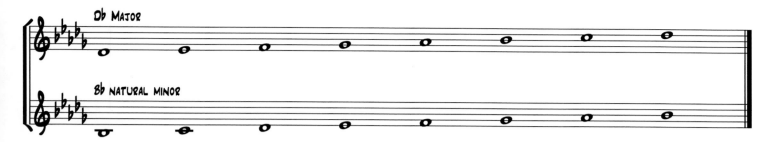

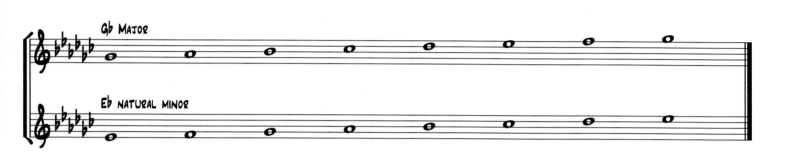

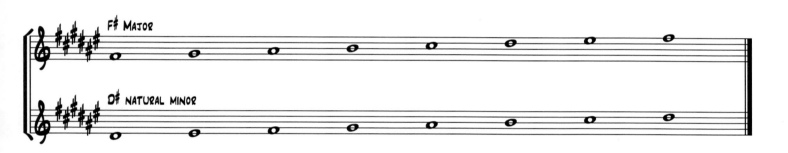

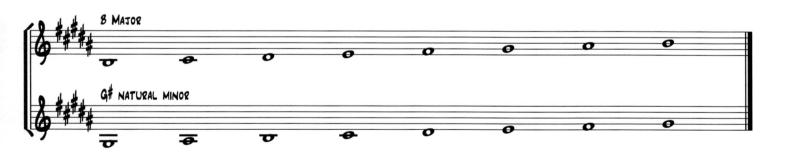

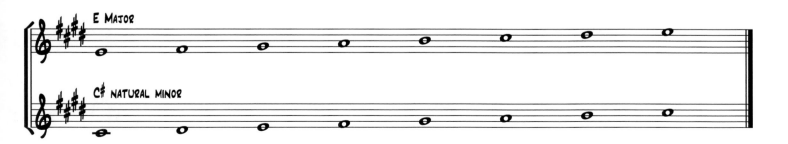

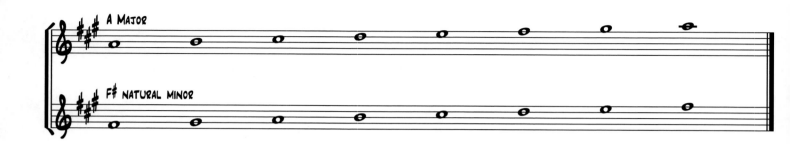

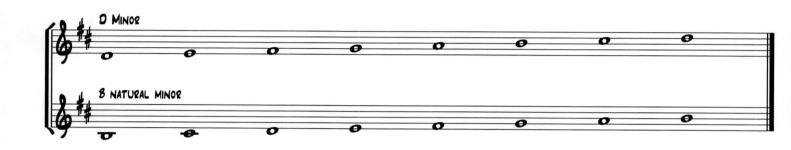

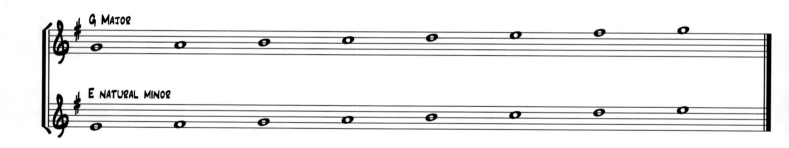

Other Minor Scales

appendix II JAZZ CHORDS LIBRARY

Chord Symbol	Chord Type	Commonly used Extensions	Chord Symbol Variations
C^6	major 6th	9, #11	$Cadd^6$
$CMAJ^7$	major 7th	9, #11, 13	$C\Delta$, Cma^7, CM^7, $Cmaj^7$
C^7	dominant 7th	9, ♭9, #11, 13, ♭13	$Cdom.^7$
C^7SUS	suspended	9, ♭9, 13	C^7sus4, $Csus4$
CM^6	minor 6th	9, 11	Cm^6, Cmi^6, $Cmin^6$, $C{-}add6$
CM^7	minor 7th	9, 11, 13	Cm^7, Cmi^7, $Cmin^7$
$CM(MAJ^7)$	minor-major 7th	9, 11, 13	$C{-}\Delta$, $Cm\Delta^7$, $Cmi^{(ma7)}$, $Cmin^{(+7)}$
$C^{\o7}$	half diminished 7th	9, 11	$C{-}^{7\,(\flat5)}$, $Cm^{7\,(\flat5)}$, $Cmi^{7\,(\flat5)}$, Cm^{7-5}, $C^{\o}$
C^{o7}	diminished 7th	any note a whole step above any chord tone	$Cdim^7$

Other Common Chord Symbols

Chord Symbol	Chord Type	Chord Symbol Variations
C+7	augmented 7th	$C^{7(\sharp 5)}$, C aug^7
C9	short hand for C dominant 7th with an added 9	C7(9), C7 (add9)
D/C7	short hand for C dominant 7th with a 9, $\sharp$11, 13. It is referred to as a "polychord."	C^{13}, $C^9(^{13}_{\sharp 11})$, $C7(^{13}_{\sharp 11})_9$
C6/G	short hand for C6 with G in the bass	C^{add6}/G
C6/9	short hand for C6 with an added 9	$C^{add6(9)}$
C7ALT	short hand for C7 with an added $\flat$9, $\sharp$9, or $\flat$13	$C^{7(\flat 9)}$, $C^{7(\sharp 9)}$, $C^{7(\flat 13)}$, $C^{7(^{\flat 13}_{\flat 9})}$

appendix III PROFESSIONAL RESOURCE GUIDE

The following is a recommended listing of books, recordings, computer programs and reference materials which may be useful to you as a jazz singer. They are all readily available through music retail stores. It is not intended to be a comprehensive list representing all quality materials that are available—actually there are so many good educational materials in existence that it would be impossible to review and catalog them all! The purpose of this section is to provide a place to start, as you continue your exploration into the artistry and mastery of jazz singing.

Recorded Sing-Along Accompaniments

Jamey Aebersold Series (Jamey Aebersold Jazz)
The original jazz play-along recordings used by jazz musicians worldwide. There are over 100 different book/CD products available. Their first-ever volume specifically designed for singers is called "It Had to Be You," Volume 107.

www.jazzbooks.com

Choice Standards (Sher Music Co.)
This 11-song CD features great standards for practice.

www.shermusic.com

Computer Sing-Along Programs

Band in a Box (PG Music)
This computer program will play songs in any key, tempo and groove that you specify. Type in the chord changes to each song, and edit them as you wish. An added advantage is that it can print out simple lead sheets.

www.pgmusic.com

Smart Music (Coda Music Technologies)
Licensed computer accompaniments for great jazz standards that correlate with the best-selling Jamey Aebersold play-along volumes, with the bonus of allowing you to adjust the tempo and key.

www.smartmusic.com

Computer Music Notation Programs

Computer software is constantly being upgraded; check system requirements before making a purchase.

Finale (Coda Music Technologies)
A complete professional music notation program, with several easy-to-learn spin-off products. For lead-sheet writing, I recommend their PrintMusic program, or try Notepad, a small program that can produce very simple lead sheets—Notepad can be downloaded for free at either:

www.finalenotepad.com or www.makemusic.com

Sibelius (Sibelius Group)
A music notation program with capabilities similar to Finale. Some say the scanning capability is of better quality than other music notation programs.

www.sibelius.com

Computer Online Music Downloads

iTunes (Apple Corporation)
Using a portable ipod, Mac or Windows computer, you can download licensed recordings of individual tunes through iTunes Music Store for a cost, per tune!

www.apple.com

Computer Online Sheet Music

Many retail music stores offer legal sheet music download services in cooperation with print music publishers. Check your local retailer's website and support your local music store. The following websites are also good resources:

www.sheetmusicdirect.com
Mostly featuring sheet music published by Hal Leonard.

www.sunhawk.com
Mostly featuring sheet music published by Warner Bros. Publications.

General Music Theory Books

Essentials of Music Theory, Complete
by Andrew Surmani, Karen Farnum Surmani and Morton Manus (Alfred Publishing)

A well-paced 120-page basic music theory work-book beginning with staff, notes and pitches and progressing through triads, inversions, and basic chord progressions. Computer software also available.

www.alfred.com

General Piano Books

Adult All-In-One Course, Volumes 1, 2 and 3
by Willard A. Palmer, Morton Manus and Amanda Vick Lethco (Alfred Publishing)

This series features a well-sequenced combination of theory and piano technique (CD Included).

www.alfred.com

Jazz Theory Books

Jazz Improvisation: A Pocket Guide
by Dan Haerle (Jamey Aebersold Jazz)

This is truly a pocket book: small enough to take with you anywhere. It is a wonderful handy resource for jazz theory and improvisation.

www.jazzbooks.com

Jazz Language, Theory & Text for Jazz Composition and Improvisation
By Dan Haerle (Warner Bros. Publications)

Dan Haerle explains jazz theory in a very clear, understandable way in this practical reference guide.

www.warnerbrospub.com

Jazz Theory Book
by Mark Levine (Sher Music)

A comprehensive jazz theory reference book with detailed explanation of jazz scales, harmony and reharmonization.

www.shermusic.com

Jazz Piano Books

Jazz Keyboard Harmony
by Noah Baerman (Alfred Publishing)

A well conceived and thorough book for learning jazz piano.

www.alfred.com

The Jazz Piano Book
by Mark Levine (Sher Music)

This book is extremely popular and has become somewhat of a classic. Covers intervals, chords, ii-V-I, jazz piano voicings and comping.

www.shermusic.com

Jazz Fake Books

The Standards Real Book (Sher Music)
Great tunes, great changes with optional alternate changes, and the verses to songs are included. This is a fabulous fake book.

www.shermusic.com

Jazz Standards: Paperback Songs (Hal Leonard)
This paperback-sized book is extremely convenient because of its small size and great tunes. As with many fakebooks, you might need to double-check some of the chord changes for accuracy! Hal Leonard also publishes full-size fakebooks.

www.halleonard.com

Just Standards Fakebook (Warner Bros. Publications)
A good compilation of jazz standards published by Warner Bros. with suggested chord substitutions.

www.warnerbrospub.com

Latin Real Book (Sher Music)
A great fakebook of classic and contemporary salsa, Latin jazz and Brazilian standards with suggested bass lines, piano montunos and horn lines. Lyrics are in Spanish, Portuguese and/or English. A sampler CD is available.

www.shermusic.com

The New Real Book, Volumes I, II and III (Sher Music)
These three editions each have different songs. All of the Sher Music books have reliable chord changes. A big plus!

www.shermusic.com

Sing Jazz!
Compiled by Dr. Gloria Cooper (Second Floor Music/ Hal Leonard Corp.)

This book is full of "off the beaten path," interesting and more contemporary jazz tunes. Worth taking a look at when searching for fresh material.

www.halleonard.com

Vocal Technique Books

The Structure of Singing: System and Art of Vocal Technique
by Richard Miller (Wadsworth)

Richard Miller's work is extremely well regarded by vocal pedagogues.

www.wadsworth.com

Singing for the Stars
by Seth Riggs (Alfred Publishing)

Seth is a world-renown teacher of singing for styles ranging from classical to rock. CD included.

www.alfred.com

Basics of Vocal Pedagogy
by Clifton Ware (McGraw-Hill Education)

Complete overview of vocal technique and pedagogy, presented in an easy to understand way.

www.McGraw-Hill.com

The Rock-N-Roll Singer's Survival Manual
by Mark Baxter (Hal Leonard)

Don't be scared off by the term "rock-n-roll," this is a great book for any singer! Very clear, common sense tips and information about healthy care of the voice, and basic technique. Also provides very interesting sections on the psychology of singing, handling performance anxiety, and professional recording situations.

www.halleonard.com

Jazz Singing Books

The Professional Vocalist: A Handbook for Commercial Singers and Teachers
by Rachel L. Lebon   (Scarecrow Press, Inc.)

This book contains a wealth of well-written information, not only about the voice, but about all aspects of being a professional vocalist in a variety of musical styles.

www.scarecrowpress.com

Sing Your Story: A Practical Guide for Learning and Teaching the Art of Jazz Singing
by Jay Clayton (Advance Music)

Ideas and tips of all kinds for jazz singers, including a helpful chapter on the business of music (CD Included).

www.advancemusic.com

The Complete Guide to Teaching Vocal Jazz
by Steve Zegree (Heritage Music Press)

This book is primarily geared toward vocal ensembles, but also contains much useful information for solo jazz singers including song interpretation, vocal improvisation, lead-sheet writing and a thorough discography (CD Included).

www.lorenz.com

Vocal Improvisation Books

Vocal Improvisation
by Michele Weir (Advance Music)

A comprehensive book with a large array of specific exercises for improvisation, information on theory, chords, progressions and playing jazz piano. Includes a glossary, discography, interviews with jazz singers, and suggested activities for use in the classroom (CD included).

www.advancemusic.com

Chet Baker's Greatest Scat Solos
Transcribed by Jim Bastian (Coastal Publishing)

Each transcribed solo contains written scat syllables underneath the pitches.

www.coastaljazz.net

Hear It and Sing It!: Exploring Modal Jazz
by Judy Niemack (Second Floor Music)

This new release contains a wealth of theoretical information and exercises for a modal (scalar) approach to jazz scatting (CD Included).

www.halleonard.com

Jazz Conception for Scat Vocal
by Jim Snidero (Advance Music)

Includes 21 solo etudes for scat singing, jazz phrasing, interpretation and improvisation based on chord changes to standards and blues, in progressive order of difficulty (CD included).

www.advancemusic.com

Scat! Vocal Improvisation Techniques
by Bob Stoloff (Gerard and Sarzin)

A useful book on vocal improvisation with numerous exercises, transcribed solos, vocal bass lines, drum grooves and more. The CD includes call and response exercises, demonstrations and sing-along chord patterns in Latin, jazz and hip-hop styles.

www.changingtones.com

**21 Bebop Exercises for Vocalists
and Instrumentalists**
by Steve Rawlins (Hal Leonard)

A useful manual for jazz vocalists who wish to explore bebop phrasing and practice in all twelve keys (CD included).

www.halleonard.com

Philosophy of Music and Performing

**The Artist's Way: A Spiritual Path
to Higher Creativity**
by Julia Cameron with Mark Bryan (Tarcher/Penguin)

Very helpful thoughts and exercises for unleashing your creative flow.

www.penguinputnam.com

**Effortless Mastery: Liberating the
Master Musician Within**
by Kenny Werner (Jamey Aebersold Jazz)

Kenny Werner is a master player, and this is a must read book! (CD included)

www.jazzbooks.com

The Inner Game of Music
by Barry Green with W. Timothy Gallwey
(Doubleday)

A musician's version of the classic *The Inner Game of Tennis* with suggestions to improve concentration, reduce nervousness and get your self-critical inner voice out of "the game!"

www.randomhouse.com/doubleday/

Self-Portrait of an Artist
by Dave Liebman (Advance Music)

Wonderful insights, techniques, and philosophies about playing jazz.

www.advancemusic.com

**How to Talk to Any Group and Sound Good No
Matter How Scared You Are**
by Peter Desberg (Square One)

Strategies to overcome the psychological effects of stagefright and performance anxiety. Includes techniques to deal with the unique physical problems experienced by musicians performing under pressure.

www.squareonepublishers.com

Rhythm Section Books

**The Jazz Director's Guide to the
Rhythm Section**

by Steve Houghton, Shelly Berg, Fred Hamilton, Lou Fischer (Alfred Publishing)

A must-have book for directors of instrumental jazz ensembles, small group combos or vocal jazz ensembles. Each chapter includes an introduction of the style, a "clinics room" that includes performance tips of the genre and a play-along piece at the end that coincides with the CD and optional DVD.

www.alfred.com

Essential Styles, Books 1 and 2
by Steve Houghton and Tom Warrington
(Alfred Publishing)

Two volumes of play-along jazz grooves for drummers and bassists; also useful for style reference for vocalists and arrangers (CD Included).

www.alfred.com

Inside the Brazilian Rhythm Section
by Nelson Faria and Cliff Korman (Sher Music)

A fabulous resource for learning about Brazilian music. Features information on eight of the most common Brazilian styles (CD Included).

www.shermusic.com

The Salsa Guidebook for Piano and Ensemble
by Rebeca Mauleon (Sher Music)

Contains 260 pages of musical examples for piano, bass, drumset and salsa percussion instruments. A good resource for exploring salsa styles.

www.shermusic.com

Jazz Reference Books

All Music Guide to Jazz
Edited by Vladimir Bogdanov, Chris Woodstra, Stephen T. Erlewine (Backbeat Books)

An excellent reference book that reviews and rates 18,000 recordings by 1,700 musicians, from early New Orleans jazz through today's recording artists. Includes concise biographies and historical information.

www.backbeatbooks.com

appendix  INDEX

Glossary & Index of Terms & Symbols

Includes all the terms and symbols used in the *Jazz Singer's Handbook* and the page on which they are first introduced and/or defined.

"A" SECTION: the first section of a song (which usually recurs); used in reference to song form designations such as AABA and ABAC (p. 42).

ARPEGGIATED MELODIC LINE: melody that moves by skips, outlining chord tones (p. 31).

AXE: slang for instrument (p. 43).

"B" SECTION: the second section of a song, occurring after the "A" section. Used in reference to song form designations such as AABA and ABAC (p. 42).

BACK BEAT: strong playing by the drummer of beats two and four in a swing feel to generate a stronger feeling of rhythmic drive (p. 78).

BACK PHRASING: delaying the start of a phrase by a couple of beats or more from its original starting point (p. 33).

BAR: slang for measure (p. 41).

BLUES: a 12-bar song form and chord progression frequently used by jazz and rock musicians (p. 43).

BREAK: all players stop playing for a measure or two, on a predetermined beat. The break starts with the playing of a strongly accented chord, most often occurring on beat one or the "and" of beat four. Often an improvisation soloist will begin his or her solo during "the break." (p. 62).

BRIDGE: the "B" section of a song that is in AABA form (p. 42).

CHANGES: short for "chord changes" (p. 49).

CHART: a lead sheet that contains arranging elements such as an intro, endings and/or rhythmic kicks (p. 51).

CHORUS: one full time through the chord progression of a song, e.g., jazz musicians "take a solo chorus" (p. 42).

CHROMATIC-APPROACH NOTE: neighbor note that precedes another note from a half step below or above (p. 31).

CODA: an added section of music, usually occurring only once at the end of an arranged song. The coda section typically contains a tag or other type of ending (p. 60).

CODA SIGN: ⊕ used to identify the coda section (p. 60).

COMP: slang for *accompanying* or *complementing*. The playing of rootless chord voicings by piano or guitar as accompaniment to a soloist when the bassist plays chord roots (p. 77).

COUNT-OFF: The counting of numbers in rhythm to establish a tempo and begin a song with a group of musicians, e.g., "1 (rest), 2 (rest), 1, 2, 3, 4" (p. 76).

CROSS STICK: hitting the rim of the snare drum with the middle (approx. 1 ½ to 2 inches from the butt end) of the drumstick as a regular part of a drum pattern (p. 78).

CUE: a hand or other visual signal during the performance of a song to communicate musical information to other performers such as the beginning of a new section, solo, or return to the head (p. 83).

D. C. (DA CAPO): repeat to the beginning of the song or arrangement (p. 60).

D. C. al FINE: repeat to the beginning of the song or arrangement and play to the end of the piece as designated by "Fine."

D. S. (DAL SEGNO): repeat to the sign 𝄋 (p. 60).

D. S. al CODA: repeat to the sign [𝄋] and play to [⊕], then skip to the Coda section [⊕] (p. 61).

D. S. al FINE: repeat to the sign [𝄋] and play to the end (Fine).

DOUBLE TIME: a change in tempo that is twice as fast as the previous tempo (p. 63).

DOUBLE-TIME FEEL: a tempo that *feels* twice as fast as the actual rate of speed of the chords and melody. Chords and melody progress as written, but the underlying rhythmic feel is double-time (p. 63).

1st and 2nd ENDINGS: play or sing through the 1st ending to the repeat sign, then go back to the beginning (or the corresponding repeat sign). On the second time through the passage, skip over the 1st ending and go directly to the 2nd (pp. 47 & 61).

EVEN EIGHTHS: see straight eighths.

EXTENSIONS: the ninth, eleventh or thirteenth scale degrees. Extensions are commonly added to chords for interest and color (p. 89).

FAKE BOOK: a compilation of lead sheets notating melody, chord symbols, and lyrics if applicable (p. 41).

FORM: see song form (p. 41).

FORWARD PHRASING: beginning a phrase at an earlier starting point than originally written (p. 34).

4-FEEL: swing feel where the bassist plays a walking bass line, and there is a driving feeling of four beats per measure (pp. 67 & 77).

GIG: slang for professional music performance, usually referring to a performance in a club or private party (p. 7).

GIG BOOK: an organized book of lead sheets and simple charts, cross-referenced by title, style and key (p. 74).

GROOVE: 1. to sing or play with a good rhythmic feel; to lock into the same rhythmic subdivision as the other players/singers during a song (p. 37); 2. rhythmic style, such as swing or bossa nova (p. 37).

HALF TIME: a change in tempo that is twice as slow as the previous tempo (p. 63).

HALF-TIME FEEL: a tempo that feels twice as slow as the actual rate of speed of the chords and melody. Chords and melody progress as written, but the underlying rhythmic feel is half time (p. 63).

HEAD: the melody of a complete song form, e.g. "Play the head" (p. 83).

IMPROVISATION: in a jazz context, spontaneous composition based on the existing chord changes of a song (p. 83).

INFLECTION: slight bending of a note up or down to another note (p. 29).

INTRO: short for introduction; music that is played before the melody to set up the style and mood of the song (p. 51).

JAZZ STANDARDS: well-known, commonly performed songs in the repertoire of most professional jazz musicians, generally written prior to the 1960s, often originally composed for Broadway or motion pictures (p. 41).

KICK: a specific rhythm played by the drummer and/or all of the rhythm section players, as brief as a single eighth note, or as long as two measures or more. Rhythmic kicks are notated with slashes (representing beats) and stems (pp. 54 & 62).

LAYING BACK: the placement of rhythms very slightly behind (on the back side) of each steady quarter-note beat (p. 37).

LEAD SHEET: music that is notated with melody, chord symbols, and if applicable, lyrics (pp. 8 & 45).

LICK: a short melodic motif, often repeated several times.

MELISMA: the singing of various notes on a single syllable or word. Sarah Vaughan used melisma extensively in her singing (p. 32).

MODULATION: changing from one key to another within a song or arrangement (p. 64).

NEIGHBOR NOTE: the note that is adjacent (by half step or whole step) to another note (p. 31).

OCTAVE DISPLACEMENT: melodic shift of a phrase or part of a phrase one octave higher or lower (p. 31).

OFF-BEAT: the weak beats of a measure, such as the "ands" of the beat in a series of eighth notes. Often, off-beats are emphasized in jazz (pp. 36 & 38).

ORNAMENTATION: decoration of a note with a series of inflections, or by surrounding the note, melodically (p. 29).

PASSING NOTE: melodic passage where a note of the scale occurs between two chord tones (p. 31).

PEDAL TONE: a single bass note, usually the root or the fifth of the key center, which remains constant underneath various changing chords above (p. 54).

PHRASING: 1. the placement of melodic phrases in relationship to their original written starting and ending points (see back phrasing and forward phrasing) (p. 33). 2. the manner in which a melody and text is delivered, especially in terms of the conversational quality and use of word stress (p. 35).

PHRASING OVER THE BAR LINE: suspension of a phrase or phrases over the predictable 2-, 4-, or 8-bar divisions of the original phrase structure of a song, often a natural result of using back or forward phrasing (p. 34).

PICKUPS: pickups are melodic notes that occur before the first full measure of a phrase. For example, the first three notes of "Autumn Leaves" are pickups ("anacrusis" in classical music) (p. 46).

PREACH-SINGING: periodic interjection of phrases, extraordinarily talkative in spirit and completely out of the groove, reminiscent of a preacher giving a passionate sermon (p. 39).

RAILROAD TRACKS: two little lines at a slant that indicate for the rhythm section to pause momentarily [//] ("caesura" in classical music) (p. 60).

REHARMONIZE: making creative alterations in the chord changes of a song (p. 70).

RHYTHM CHANGES: slang referring to the popular chord progression to "I've Got Rhythm".

RHYTHMIC BREAK: see break.

RHYTHMIC KICK: see kick.

RIDE PATTERN: a specific rhythm that jazz drummers play on the ride cymbal when in swing feel (p. 78).

RIM SHOT: a short and loud "crack," sounded by hitting the drum so the stick strikes the drumhead and rim simultaneously (p. 78).

ROOT: the tonic note of a chord (p. 77).

RUBATO: no tempo (p. 35).

SCAT SINGING: vocal improvisation using syllables (p. 83).

SLASHES: slanted lines positioned in each measure of a rhythm section lead sheet to indicate beats and chord alignment (p. 45).

SITTING IN: unrehearsed performance where you are invited to sing a song or two on someone else's gig, or where you are participating in an organized jam session (p. 82).

SOLO: improvisation of new melodic lines to the chord progression of a song (p. 83).

SONG FORM: the organizational structure of a song, e.g., AABA (p. 41).

STANDARDS: see jazz standards.

STRAIGHT EIGHTH NOTES: eighth notes that are performed with a "normal," even subdivision, rather than the underlying triplet feeling of swing (also called "even eighths") (p. 79).

STOP TIME: passage of music played with a series of rhythmic breaks (p. 81).

SWING EIGHTHS NOTES: eighth notes that are interpreted as a triplet with the first two notes tied, a fundamental aspect of swing feel (p. 36).

SYNCOPATION: rhythmic emphasis on the weak beats of a measure, such as beats two and four in 4/4 (p. 36).

TAG: the repetition of the last phrase of a song, most commonly two or three times (p. 57).

TONE COLOR: different timbres of the voice that help express emotion, e.g., rich and warm, bright and focused (p. 29).

TRANSPOSING: the process of changing a song's key from one to another (p. 48).

TURNAROUND: short chord progression that cycles through the circle of 5ths (p. 51).

2 FEEL: swing feel where the bassist plays roots, or roots and 5ths of the chords on beats one and three only, giving the music a feeling of two beats per measure (pp. 67 & 77).

VAMP: two or three chords repeated four or more times, most often used for intros and endings (pp. 52 & 59).

VERSE: in jazz standard song forms, an introductory passage occurring before the main body (chorus) of the song, usually performed rubato (p. 42).

VOCALESE: the performance of a previously recorded instrumental solo with the addition of lyrics.

VOICING: the arrangement of chord tones and extensions as played by a pianist or guitar player (p. 77).

WALKING BASS LINE: characterized by the predominant use of four quarter notes in each measure. Walking bass lines are in "4" (p. 77).